The International Series in

FOUNDATIONS OF EDUCATION

Consulting Editor

HERBERT M. KLIEBARD
University of Wisconsin

*Cultural Pluralism
and American
Education*

Cultural Pluralism and American Education

SEYMOUR W. ITZKOFF

Department of Education and Child Study
Smith College
Northampton, Massachusetts

INTERNATIONAL TEXTBOOK COMPANY

Scranton, Pennsylvania

Standard Book Number 7002 2216 2

Copyright ©, 1969, by International Textbook Company

Library of Congress Catalog Card Number: 70—86866

To Pat

Preface

Cultural Pluralism and American Education is an essay in the social and philosophical foundations of education. It reflects a concern for the changing character of our society and the manner in which formal education has become enmeshed in its institutional patterns. Philosophically, it is an attempt to find new intellectual roots for the theory of cultural pluralism. Our hope is that these views will contribute to the continuing dialogue in education.

The idea of cultural pluralism is of course the creative inspiration of Horace Kallen. And it has fallen to him to argue for and promulgate it in his various writings. I will always be indebted for a conversation I had with him several years ago about this and other topics, as well as for his written encouragement in the intervening years. I. B. Berkson figures importantly in the development of the pluralistic approach to society and a richly humanistic interpretation of education throughout his career. His wise friendship over the years has been a resource of inestimable value to me as well as to others beginning their philosophical careers in education.

R. Freeman Butts and Philip H. Phenix gave invaluable counsel and criticism to an earlier draft of this manuscript. I am especially indebted to Dr. Phenix for his insistence on the need for clarity in philosophical writing. What there is here in the way of succinctness is certainly due to his guidance. For deviations from the mark, I must of course be responsible. For the hours of editorial work that have given this study a semblance of literary order, I thank my wife, to whom this book is dedicated.

Seymour W. Itzkoff

June, 1969
Northampton, Massachusetts

Contents

What America is witnessing is a new kind of clustering together of ethnic groups, who are perhaps frightened of being isolated from that which is familiar and reassuring. In a society that seems to be spinning apart, one's own special identity becomes essential to survival.

Paul Jacobs and Saul Landau
The Center Magazine, March 1969

For law is order, and good law is good order; but a very great multitude cannot be orderly: to introduce order into the unlimited is the work of a divine power—of such a power as holds together the universe. Beauty is realized in number and magnitude, the state which combines magnitude with good order must necessarily be the most beautiful. To the size of states there is a limit, as there is to other things, plants, animals, implements; for none of these retain their natural power when they are too large or too small, but they either wholly lose their nature, or are spoiled.

Aristotle: Politics
Ca. 340 B. C.

Introduction

The major social problems of our time have been induced by the impact of the mass technological society on the existing institutional structure. With inexorable force, scientific technology has worked its way into virtually every corner of our earth. Wherever it has lodged itself, in the space of a generation it has transformed the traditional relationships of man to man. In turn, these transformations have altered the content and form of our educational institutions.

However, it is not enough to speak of these changes in terms of technology and economics. Perhaps these are primary and causative. Inevitably, these new structural conditions have brought about radical changes in the qualitative dimensions of our political and social life. The proliferation of material complexity and people has resulted in a shift of power to more centralized controls. The rapid changes in all of these social and technical factors have necessitated that we either manage, control, and order our world, or dissolve in anarchy and chaos.

In just a few generations, we have experienced the slow but steady diminution of individual choice, initiative, and privacy, increasing cultural homogeneity, bureaucratization, and the externalization of personal relationships. The moral, religious, and ethnic values of the past have been rendered irrelevant in the face of this set of social dynamics. Their disintegration in the absence of rational alternatives has resulted in an educational tradition largely bereft of philosophical direction. The institutional hierarchy in education seems to float from one current and inevitably transient enthusiasm to the next, always awaiting its cues from the outside.

Simply put, our argument is that the mass society cannot work. Man will never freely assent to the social, moral, and educational values that are produced from its structure. In short, it is subversive to the most basic requirements of cultural existence. The first chapter presents evidence for this claim. It is devoted to a delineation of several of the negative by-products of our current trend towards massiveness and centralization. We argue that the institutions of formal education, always sensitive to the needs of modernity, have themselves been neutralized insofar as they might provide the critical distance necessary to evaluate constructively the trends of our era.

In Chapter 2 we expand upon our contemporary diagnosis of the problem by examining historically some intellectual patterns that have been considered and abandoned as we have gradually blundered into our present dilemma. The philosophy of cultural pluralism is one such pattern. It is an approach to social organization that is useful to study, both as a revelation of the past and as a possible guide for the future.

We note that in the early part of our century, a number of philosophers and educators promoted this system of values as the most democratic solution to the challenges we faced in the tide of immigration that America had to absorb from 1870 on. Cultural pluralism was particularly appropriate, since most of the immigrants were of non-Anglo-Saxon ethnic stock. This movement was supported by John Dewey, then the great spokesman of progressivism in education and social democracy. But while the pluralists, led by Horace Kallen, raised their voices in philosophical argument with the Anglo-Saxon chauvinists and the melting-pot assimilationists, they clearly were defeated in their attempts to establish social roots for their views of a pluralistic democracy.

Horace Kallen had defiantly predicted the ultimate vindication of pluralism. But its gradual dissipation in the decades between 1920 and 1950 is generally recognized. Yet, even under the most unfavorable social conditions, there have been some minorities that have continued their cultural associations and, as a result, still maintain a semblance of identity.[1] Originally, the philosophy of cultural pluralism drew much of its impetus from John Dewey's views on human nature, democ-

---

[1] Nathan Glazer and Daniel Moynihan, *Beyond the Melting Pot* (Cambridge, Mass.: M. I. T. Press, 1963).

racy, and community. However, we argue that the inherent omissions and weaknesses in this philosophy, especially in its conception of human nature and culture, sapped the intellectual strength of the movement and clouded the climate of opinion that could have lent it greater social credence.

Thus it is that the intellectual clue to the weaknesses in the pluralistic movement of the early decades of our century provides a key to understanding our present philosophical flaccidity in opposing some of the more execrable characteristics of current society. Cultural pluralism was inherently right for the early twentieth century and it is right for us today, even if its character will of necessity be different. We contend that it constitutes an antidote to and possibly an alternative for the mass society. But to understand both illness and remedy, we must explore new intellectual resources and establish other philosophical guidelines.

In Chapter 3, we turn to the philosophy of Ernst Cassirer. His views on human nature, knowledge, and culture appear to confirm our belief that pluralism is indeed a natural cultural condition, one under which men have lived since the beginning of society itself. Crucial to Cassirer's arguments are (a) the neo-Kantian philosophy of critical idealism in knowledge, (b) the conception of man as *animal symbolicum* (the symbolic animal), and finally (c) the intellectual recognition of the legitimacy of a wide variety of symbolic and cultural expression. The neo-Kantians attempted to rectify traditional views that knowledge is imposed upon man by some external structure of reality. Cassirer viewed knowledge as a synthetic creation of man's mind, organized from the inchoate sensations of experience. Knowledge, therefore, whether in science or art, is conventional or symbolic. It takes its meaning from the spontaneous and creative act of ordering and structuring that man's mind provides in the context of culture. This view of knowledge, which in its formal claims parallels Dewey's instrumentalism, points, however, to certain unique conclusions about human nature.

Human beings are not problem-solving animals. Nor are they motivated by any specific survivalistic drives. If there is an inner dynamic drive in human action, it is the need for symbolic envisagement. Man lives in a world of his own meanings. There is no reality available to him but that presented through the particular symbols of his culture. In this position, to understand human actions we must eschew the traditional deterministic materialism of recent intellectual history and adopt a more sophisticated interpretation of human motivations.

Culture cannot be bifurcated between the rationality of scientific thought and technological achievement, and the supposed emotive irrationality of esthetic, religious, and ethical values. All are enclosed in the circle of culture. All sets of symbolic meanings reveal man to himself. In a sense, human nature itself is created through the various structures of symbolic meaning that demarcate one culture from another and produce different kinds of persons. Although Cassirer did not write on pluralism specifically, his conception of the symbolic forms lends itself easily to such an extrapolation. What we call at various times discursive thought—the scientific or theoretical attitude—strives to overcome diversity and attain intellectual unity. This attitude of mind extends as much to social experience as it does to the physical world.

On the other hand there is a vast realm of symbolic expression in the cultural world, in religious practices, the many and various art forms and the diverse patterns of societal behavior which constitute that mysterious entity called national character, and ethnicity. The meanings of this world of non-discursive symbols are not generally communicable. They do not point to any stable set of references existing outside the culture. Their locus is within the culture as a self-satisfying structure of meaning and signification.

Science searches for larger relationships, for unity in the diversity of experience. It is facilitated in this quest by the fact that all men confront the same physical structure of things. The non-discursive flourishes in the context of diversity. Whereas we may compare variant theories of physics, or even economics, in terms of truth or falsehood, the cultural patterns of art, humor, and cuisine do not transcend the barriers of culture. They are incomparable in terms of an external standard of value.

We argue that the historic cultural diversity of man is not accidental or aberrant. It is, on the contrary, a manifestation of a universal symbolic need experienced in society. If this contention is correct, then we ought to be able to translate a philosophical position on pluralism into a relevant theory of the democratic life. We are obliged to put it forward in the context of the present sweep toward cultural conformity.

In Chapter 4 we argue that the relevance of the theoretical roots of pluralism for a theory of democracy lies in the clarification of the issues of equality and similarity in society. Too often differences in culture have been used as weapons. This has led to a natural fear that pluralism perpetuates inequality. By distinguishing between caste differences—the result of the power to coerce—and inherent differences in cultural behavior, we could disarm the power element in cultural differentiation. This could result in a world in which men would be equal, yet free to be different.

This necessitates a careful rational analysis within each society of the problem of power and differentiation, to discover intrinsic cultural diversities and those which are merely reflections of the inequalities in the power to choose. Here we do not attempt, as is done in physical theory, to neutralize qualitative differences in order to effect a unity of thought. Rather the focus is on creating uniformity of power which becomes prologue to the achievement of fundamental freedoms. These freedoms are then expressed in the *diverse* cultural choices which men naturally would wish to make.

Because of the current symbolism of national unity in our own culture, equality now necessitates conformity, the very opposite of what a free society should aim to achieve. The analysis we will make through the insights provided by our symbolic philosophy leads to some sobering conclusions about the use of power in our democratic society. It also leads to rather unusual suggestions concerning a number of important contemporary social and educational issues. In Chapter 5 we turn to these concrete matters.

The results of this analysis indicate that, seen in its long range implications, the complete integration of the black American and other minorities is less than the democratic panacea it has long appeared to be. Ultimately integration, as predicted on the basis of our position, would not benefit the black community. On the contrary, it would lead to its extirpation and the loss of vital diversity necessary to our cultural environment.

Recent developments would indicate that black people as well as other minorities—Latin American and Indians—are today sensitive to these rights and needs.

An analysis of the curriculum, of our public school organization, and of the changing character of private education leads us to conclude that a radical revision of many of our traditional assumptions about public education may be necessary. We will argue that the evolving character of the public school curriculum as well as the internal administrative orientation of the schools has made it impossible to deal with the most important human questions of values. What has resulted is an educational enterprise that is immersed in some of the more detestable qualities of our mass culture.

While we cannot argue that our salvation to these larger social problems lies solely in the schools, we do maintain that an important contribution to the general structural health of our society can be made through education. It is at this point that we urge greater subsidization of private education, as long as the dispensing institutions remain responsive to the larger needs of society and to a commitment to equality of opportunity.

Problems of unity and diversity are then raised with regard to the international scene. A number of approaches and solutions to existing pluralistic political entities are shown to have been made by various nations. It is interesting to note that while there is the usual evidence of the extirpation of minority enclaves in favor of greater transnational unity, there are nations which are attempting to balance the various demands for unification and equality with those of autonomy and differentiation. The shibboleth that diversity, both structural and substantive, is a natural enemy of the democratic commonwealth can be dispelled by the evidence.

In the final chapter several current educational issues—student rights, private education, and decentralization and local control—are discussed from the standpoint of a pluralistic position. The concern here lies in the possibility of establishing structural conditions for the natural and healthy growth of diversity. As a general condition for the achievement of these ends, we discuss what constitutes the great nemesis and obstacle of our time—the population explosion. As a social issue this takes priority over every problem, with the exception of the threat of atomic war. Our position is simply that we must put an end to the unchecked proliferation of people. We must bend all of our discursive rational and institutional efforts toward reversing our catastrophic demographic trend. Democratic pluralism and its educational correlates are seen as impossibilities when confronted by the rising tide of people. The physical as well as the social resources necessary to organize and stabilize this inchoate mass will inevitably drain away all of our surplus energies.

Our ultimate goal for a world society is the equality of men, not their uniformity. Our hope is that an educational enterprise that is worthwhile will bring us closer to the point where we can face practical issues of social change with intelligence. With the establishment of the principle of equality and the requisite reason to guide our choices, we might expect that the pluralistic vision of culture would prevail. Man would then be able to engage in the most creative and diverse symbolic endeavors without fear of loss of social status—power. This might well be the aim of all educational ventures: to enable us to regulate the external relations of man so that his deeper cultural capacities may be liberated and fully explored.

chapter 1

The Contemporary
Context of Education

EDUCATION AND THE DEMOCRATIC IDEAL

The concept of democracy has been the most significant symbol through which the American mission has been defined. Its meaning has not only been enriched by the historic record of achievements of our people but it has signified the existence of a set of ideals and values that we consciously pursue into the future. Traditionally, democracy has been conceived as a body of law and practice that protects the individual, in the free pursuit of his natural inclinations, from the encroachments of the various institutions of society.

In recent times we have begun to redefine the nature of the democratic commitment. Though law and constitutionalism,— the checks and balances so crucial for preventing too much power from accruing to any particular group,—are important, other more substantive qualities of democracy have come to be recognized. The Bill of Rights, certainly the foundation stone of our democracy, has been made richer by the implicit assumption of our people that its formal guarantees are unimportant, if not even impotent, if these are not correlated with a conviction that democracy is inextricably involved in a commitment to the good life.

The guarantees of the Constitution are thus more than negative inhibitions against actions inimical to man's freedom. They are prelude, even goad, toward the establishment by our people of social forms and institutions through which man can exercise his natural desires consonant with his social nature.

It was this broadened view of the democratic enterprise that characterized the intellectual activities of modern theorists such as Thorstein Veblen, Charles Beard, Oliver Wendell Holmes, James Harvey Robinson, and especially John Dewey. Morton White has characterized their work in the various disciplines of the social sciences as "the revolt against formalism."[1] The period at the beginning of our century was a renaissance of thought, a significant redefining of the historic vision of the democratic life reminiscent of Jefferson's vision, but in a context that purported to carry us forward into the technological world we were destined to inhabit.[2]

Dewey's great contribution to the growth of democratic practice was centered in the revisions he stimulated in educational thought and action. To him, the public school was that institution most central to the translation of abstract philosophical principles into living experience. Not having any vested interests in the social status quo, it could be looked upon as an independent agency for the constant reinterpretation and revision of these values as the times made necessary. As such, it could become the pivotal institution in our society for the cultivation of pertinent values giving substance to the democratic life.[3] In spite of the historic limitations of Dewey's philosophy, the progressives were successful in reshaping the American schools. This is testimony to the fact that our society was receptive to a view that the quality of life we lead as partially shaped by our educational system is an important aspect of our national philosophy.

Had the social reformers of the early twentieth century been successful in making their views a more permanent part of our society, the educational prescriptions of the progressives might have had a more lasting impact. As it was (since education has traditionally reflected the values of society, rather than determined them as the social reconstructionists wanted), the prescriptions of this movement gradually faded into the historic landscape.

---

[1] Morton White, *Social Thought in America* (Boston: Beacon Press, 1957).

[2] Gail Kennedy, in Max Fisch (ed.), *Classic American Philosophers* (New York: Appleton-Century-Crofts, 1951), p. 328.

[3] John Dewey, *Democracy and Education* (New York: Macmillan Company, 1916).

Changing American Educational Ideals

It must not be thought that this philosophical attempt to integrate the values of a society with intellectually determinable ideals is an historically misguided ideal. The history of our nation and the educational values that have been evolved show the continuing and influential role of education in shaping the diverse value systems that have contributed to our form of society.

The Puritan schools, although an adjunct of the established church, were an integral part of the communities' philosophical purview. They were democratic only in the sense that schooling was universal in scope and intent. The intellectual and social contexts in which they were rooted would today be considered insufferable. Yet in their own time they provided those who were so educated a standard with which to confront experience successfully.[4]

When the scientific enlightenment began to infiltrate our society in the eighteenth century, giving rise to an intellectual environment that produced those revolutionists and statesmen who set us free, a new set of philosophical and educational values was interposed. The laissez-faire political and economic views of that time (1750-1825) thrust aside public education, partially because of its historic association with the centralized, theocratic New England absolutism, and the educational focus switched to the political arena.[5] It was from here that the ideals of that era were shaped. Nevertheless education, though emanating from the political forums, was deemed to be a high concern of the society in shaping and giving substance to the most advanced philosophical views of the time.[6]

Not until the nineteenth-century masses began to agitate for a greater measure of social equality do we see the reestablishment of public education. A new form of social democracy could be felt. It was once more a theistic, but humanistic intellectual movement—Transcendentalism. The social reformers

[4] Clinton Rossiter, *The First American Revolution* (New York: Harcourt, Brace & World, 1956), pp. 215-217.
[5] Merle Curti, *Social Thought in America* (New York: Littlefield, Adams & Company, 1959), pp. 35-40.
[6] Vernon L. Parrington, *Main Currents in American Thought* (New York: Harcourt, Brace & World, 1954), Vol I, p. 283.

of this era—like Thaddeus Stevens, Horace Mann, Henry Barnard—saw in the Common School the perfect vehicle for the extension of the democratic vision to a more encompassing social context than had been conceived during the time of our revolution.[7]

The progressive era proclaimed a number of innovations that greatly expanded our perception of what the democratic life was and how the now lusty public educational system might implement these new values. The concept of democracy was rooted in a philosophical context that involved new assumptions concerning human nature, scientific thought, intelligence, and community and social life. The schools were to carry out the prescriptions proclaimed by this new philosophy. And for approximately seventy years (1876-1945) our educational system alternately confronted, absorbed, and reacted to this new program. This reevaluation of the democratic ideal did not take place in education alone. There were few aspects of our political and social life that did not feel its imprint. As many legislative and social practices were born due to this revolt against the formalistic views of preceding eras as were born due to the industrial revolution.

But even this historically significant movement, having served out its moment in time, was destined to exhaust itself and, in the context of new problems that time inexorably produces, to fall away into relative obsolescence. Lawrence Cremin places its educational demise after World War II.[8] New concerns were to make a heavy impact upon American education, and even more directly upon the character and outlook of our culture.

We live today in a remarkably complex age. The rapid rate of technological innovation has brought about a corresponding increase in the rate of change in practically every area of our social experience. We now have to face a radically new condition. In previous historical periods the changes in our social experience were created by conscious alternations in the intel-

---

[7] R. Freeman Butts and Lawrence A. Cremin, *History of Education in American Culture* (New York: Holt, Rinehart & Winston, Inc, 1953), p. 202.

[8] Lawrence A. Cremin, *The Transformation of the School* (New York: Alfred A. Knopf, Inc., 1961), pp. 267-270.

lectual climate. Our own era, by contrast, has experienced such dizzying material changes that the accompanying social changes have been precipitated without the directing controls that an understanding of these new social phenomena would have given us. As a result, such phenomena as the growth of organizational and corporate structure, the expansion of governmental and charitable institutions, the significant increase in our material standard of living, the threat of nuclear war and the seemingly uncontrolled population explosion have outrun all prior philosophical systems that purport to give man a structure of ideas through which he can organize intellectually his social experiences.

Today the traditional questions about the nature of the good life, freedom, and reason are asked less frequently. Instead, piecemeal programs are offered to meet the immediate needs of a society facing a continuing series of social dislocations. These programs, further, are framed within a vision that is almost entirely materialistic, an economic vision hoping to fulfill what seems to be the ultimate goal of our national enterprises—prosperity and full employment.

Even our schools have been turned from their traditional concern for those larger pursuits—freedom, morality, and reason—of our democratic commitment, to the realization of the newer and more simplified values of economic affluence and technological innovation. Two gigantic wars have forced us into those patterns that have defined the contemporary world-wide context of education. In addition they have persuaded us to equate economic and technological dominance with political security. Thus if we ever hope to use our educational institutions as semiautonomous innovators and protectors of new democratic values, we must understand the larger implications of our contemporary cultural existence, its dilemmas as well as its opportunities.

We will therefore attempt to show that new social events have altered the framework within which our educational institutions must do their work. We will argue the necessity to redefine the meaning of freedom in the light of the new challenges that democracy encounters. In thus clarifying the context of our contemporary educational effort we will be in a position to reestablish a more traditional relationship between the highest intellectual and rational values of our society and the educational means by which our people can attain their historic goals.

THE COMING OF THE MASS SOCIETY

The British historian Edward Hallett Carr has perhaps most succinctly summarized these changes. In *The New Society* he shows the necessity for coming to grips with the changes in social and class structure that have occurred as a result of the historic changes of the past century and a half.[9] While he recognizes the catalyzing effect of our technological revolution, he is primarily concerned with the results in terms of economic and political revisions in the power structure.[10] By understanding the meaning of these revisions in heretofore orthodox conditions, we can better deal with the disturbed state of affairs of our own time. In general, Carr claims that our difficulties are engendered by the fact that our conception of the democratic society is conditioned by our use of intellectual tools now largely obsolete. He urges us to shed the social and political dogmas of earlier eras.

According to Carr, practically all modern democratic societies have been built on those eighteenth-century assumptions about man and society that brought the middle-class mercantilists to dominance. The bourgeoisie had taken control from the divine-right agricultural aristocracy of the previous era, in the name of a number of democratic individualistic rights that in their own day were truly revolutionary. The institutions the bourgeoisie established—political, economic, and social—were all predicated on the laissez-faire individualism that was instrumental in bringing about the revolution and bringing down the old order.[11]

Carr contends that in the context of the eighteenth century those institutional forms that predominated truly reflected man's most advanced understanding of the natural and social forces at work in human affairs. For their time, these institu-

---

[9] Edward Hallett Carr, *The New Society* (Boston: Beacon Press, 1957).
[10] *Ibid.*, p. 11.
[11] *Ibid.*, p. 62.

tions were not only revolutionary but progressive. The new social forms, as they were structured, allowed for an expansion in
a number of areas. These forms gave to history a new vision of
the meaning of individualism and democracy. Eventually they
were to create and be replaced by forms that rendered the prior
eighteenth- and nineteenth-century philosophical perspective ob-
solescent and, as we have seen, politically and morally disastrous for our own time.[12]

In the new era, Carr claims, technological advances have
brought the lowest classes of society to power, have freed them
from their previous voicelessness and, as the wave of twentieth-
century revolutions has shown, have given them a pivotal position in modern society. New philosophical visions have reinterpreted the sacrosanct assumptions concerning the nature of
individual rights as the intellectual rationalization of a class still
anxious to retain its prerogatives. More important, the economic forces, of their own inertia, have rendered the older
individualism untenable in our own era.[13]

The mass society of the twentieth century now demands
new forms of institutional living in which economic and social
rights will be extended equally to members of all strata of
society.

> For myself, it seems inconceivable that we can return to the
> individualist democracy of a privileged class; and, by the same
> token, we cannot return to the exclusively political democracy of
> the weak state exercising only police functions. We are com-
> mitted to mass democracy, to egalitarian democracy, to the pub-
> lic control and planning of the economic process, and therefore
> to the strong state exercising remedial and constructive func-
> tions.[14]

But the situation reflects much more than the problem of
merely accommodating ourselves to a world in which the masses
demand the same privileges heretofore afforded only to the
wealthy. The very conditions that have produced opportunities
for the downtrodden have also produced challenges of an entirely new sort. Carr notes that the mass society has created
organizational conditions in which the old appeal to rational

---

12 *Ibid.*, p. 21.
13 *Ibid.*, pp. 19-39.
14 *Ibid.*, p. 78.

decision making based upon well-considered philosophical assumptions is now largely absent.

The central problem which I have been discussing today touches the essence of democracy itself. Large-scale political organizations show many of the characteristics of large-scale economic organization, and have followed the same path of development. Mass democracy has, through its very nature, thrown up on all sides specialized groups of leaders—what are sometimes called elites. Everywhere, in government, in political parties, in trade unions, in co-operatives, these indispensable elites have taken shape with startling rapidity over the last thirty years. Everywhere the rift has widened between leaders and rank and file. . . . Broadly speaking, the role of reason varies inversely with the number of those to whom the argument is addressed. The decision of the leaders may be taken on rational grounds. But the motivation of the decision to the rank and file of the party or union, and still more to the general public, will contain a larger element of the irrational the larger the audience becomes. The spectacle of an efficient elite maintaining its authority and asserting its will over the mass by the rationally calculated use of irrational methods of persuasion is the most disturbing nightmare of mass democracy.[15]

Conservative Suspicion

The seriousness with which Carr evaluates the challenges to political democracy, in spite of the demonstrable democratization that has taken place in our world in both the political and economic realms, is symptomatic of the concern of thoughtful men about the character of our times. In spite of his reservations, Carr is a liberal historian with a large measure of optimism about the future, especially in the light of the great social advances that have taken place in the last several centuries.

More conservative thinkers such as T. S. Eliot and Walter Lippman have been far more pessimistic.[16,17] Their perspective is focused not upon the achievement of democratic power by the masses but upon what they see as the inevitable debasement of our social and cultural life. They are not assured that the masses, benefiting from the comforts, the security, and the

---

[15] *Ibid.*, pp. 77-78.

[16] Walter Lippman, *Essays in the Public Philosophy* (Boston: Little, Brown and Company, 1955).

[17] T. S. Eliot, *The Idea of a Christian Society* (New York: Harcourt, Brace & World, Inc., 1940).

status of our organized society, will contribute to the enhancement or preservation of human freedom.

The demurral of many conservative thinkers from the so-called liberal orthodoxy has been based upon the character of life that has resulted from the masses' thrust for control. The material security that has accrued to the masses in Western society, especially in the United States, has created social and cultural trends that, because of the vast interlocking economic structure of our society, have served to annihilate many enclaves of minority values. A thin patina of literacy and a fragile veneer of cultural enterprise tied in with concerted economic power have inaugurated an era of mass culture and leisure disseminated via the mass-communications media. The result has been less than beneficial for the traditional cultural values that have enhanced Western society. The masses have fallen prey, through the commercialization of the communications media, to the vulgarization of their cultural existence.

The mass society has thus begun to take on a character of its own. Quite rapidly, our social institutions, from the political to the religious, have begun to reflect the same qualities of salesmanship, hucksterism, and demagogy by which the attention of the masses has always been ensnared and held. The new society has begun to generate its own social evils, inevitably enveloping the traditional diversity in social life that historically permitted the generation of alternate values and expectations. If this process is allowed to continue, the conservatives argue, the malleability of these mass values and their present susceptibility to change may be lost and all alternatives effaced. Over thirty years ago, Ortega y Gasset recognized this quality of modern industrial society and spoke out eloquently against the type of human being being bred in it:

> The characteristic of the hour is that the commonplace-mind, knowing itself to be commonplace, has the assurance to proclaim the rights of the commonplace and to impose them wherever it will. As they say in the United States: "to be different is to be indecent." The mass crushes beneath it everything that is different, everything that is excellent, individual, qualified and select. Anybody who is not like everybody, who does not think like everybody, runs the risk of being eliminated. And it is clear, of course, that this "everybody" is not "everybody." "Everybody" was normally the complex unity of the mass and the divergent,

specialized minorities. Nowadays, "everybody" is the mass alone. Here we have the formidable fact of our times, described without any concealment of the brutality of its features.[18] (Italics in original.)

The question which the conservatives raise with regard to the nature of freedom does not concern itself with quantitative or participational criteria for obtaining the fruits of cultural life. Rather, their concern is with the quality of life and thus with the substantive nature of freedom. The coarseness which Ortega y Gasset and Eliot discern in the mass society can be illustrated by a multitude of contemporary social documents dealing with uniformity, materialism, delinquency, and immorality. These latter are products that attest to the recent dominance by the mass society; they also give evidence of its inevitable residue.

Sensory and Esthetic Impoverization

Let us briefly examine some of the consequences of these conditions of life that lie close to the being of each individual. Whenever the state of freedom in our society is discussed, it is rare that the sensory and perceptual dimension of life is considered pertinent to the problem. Yet, for a complete understanding of our democratic life, it is crucial. Indeed, the domination of Western culture is as much due to the West's claims of cultural hegemony as to its technological prowess.

Yet in our own century there is little doubt that accompanying the shifting locus of political and social power there has been a qualitative change in the nature of our cultural life. For the first time in the history of the West the producers of culture have felt it necessary to abjure from achieving what is the best possible expression of contemporary artistic endeavor and aim for the lowest common denominator. This has not been done to destroy artistic enterprise, merely to use art to support economics or politics. Whether it is private industry and its advertising agencies, the mass-communication industries or the political bosses of the overtly totalitarian states the result has been the same. Art has, in our society, increasingly served the aims of commerce. And since business flourishes in our culture through

[18] José Ortega y Gasset, *The Revolt of the Masses* (New York: W. W. Norton & Company, Inc., 1932), p. 19.

conducive to furthering the process of mass production and consumption, depersonalization and deindividuation. Irving Howe has expressed this subtle undermining of man's leisure patterns as follows:

> Whatever its manifest content, mass culture must therefore not subvert the basic patterns of industrial life. Leisure time must be so organized as to bear a factitious relationship to working time: apparently different, actually the same. It must provide relief from work monotony without making the return to work too unbearable; it must provide amusement without insight and pleasure without disturbance—as distinct from art which gives pleasure through disturbance.
>
> Mass culture is thus oriented toward a central aspect of industrial society: the depersonalization of the individual. On the one hand, it diverts the worker from his disturbing education to semi-robot status by arranging "relaxing" amusements for him. The need for such amusements explains the ceaseless and hectic quest for novelty in the mass-culture industries (e.g., the "Twist" in popular songs, the melodic phrase the audience remembers.) On the other hand, mass culture reinforces those emotional attitudes that seem inseparable from existence in modern society. . . . What is supposed to deflect us from the reduction of our personalities actually reinforces it.[22]

True, our perceptual life has been degraded and our culture is both artificial and cheap. Yet the essential private areas of freedom and leisure that modern technology has made possible are still available to us. We are not bowed by brute labor for infinite hours day in day out. With the exception of the cacophonic din that afflicts our ears or the urban stench out of which our lungs must sift sustenance there is still a choice of alternatives, and overall more happiness in our society than in earlier centuries.

But perhaps, as Ernest Van den Haag, a critic of the mass society, has suggested, the criterion of individual happiness is no sure test of the status of a way of life:

> There have been periods happier and others more desperate than ours. But we don't know which. And even an assertion as reasonable as this is a conjecture like any comparison of today's bliss with yesterday's. The happiness felt in disparate groups, in

[22] Irving Howe, "Notes on Mass Culture." Reprinted with permission of the Macmillan Company from Bernard Rosenberg and David M. White (eds.), *Mass Culture.* Copyright © by The Free Press, a Corporation, 1957, p. 497.

disparate periods and places cannot be measured and compared. Our contention is simply that by *distracting from the human predicament and blocking individuation and experience,* popular culture impoverishes life without leading to contentment. But whether "the mass of men" felt better or worse without the mass-production techniques of which popular culture is an ineluctable part, we shall never know. Of happiness and despair, we have no measure.[23] (Italics in original.)

The Psychological Malaise

Perhaps a more real test than that of privacy and personal happiness is the overt public expression of human behavior in the mass society. A host of psychologists, from Sigmund Freud and Karen Horney to Erich Fromm, has studied and documented the rise of mental unhealth in the urban contexts of our industrialized civilization. Indeed, Franz Alexander has stated that neurosis is the characteristic disturbance of our age.[24] But it is not our role here to delineate the etiology of the mental debilitations of our age. What we want to pursue is the issue of democracy and freedom in this new context and to test the reality of the claims of this mass democracy against the quality of life the mass of men must experience. One can argue that the system itself is as exploitive in its own way as was the industrial system of the nineteenth century which it purported to displace.

Erich Fromm touched upon it when he described the system of industrial capitalism in its psychological dimension. Robbed of real work, of a relationship between his own activities and the concerns of the society, the individual must retreat from an involvement in the work of society. He becomes prey to those emotional dependencies so characteristic of totalitarian societies.[25] Today a large portion of mankind lives under social systems whose organizational structure is so directed that individuals cannot have normal community channels for self-expression. The resulting society of voiceless masses becomes

23 Ernest Van den Haag, "Of Happiness and Despair We Have No Measure," in Rosenberg and White, *op. cit.,* p. 536.

24 Franz Alexander, *The Scope of Psychoanalysis* (New York: Basic Books, Inc. 1961), p. 173.

25 Erich Fromm, *Escape From Freedom* (New York: Farrar & Rinehart 1941), pp. 136-206.

susceptible to the most extreme and subtle social manipulations:

> Authority in the middle of the twentieth century has changed its character; it is not overt authority, but anonymous, invisible, alienated authority. Nobody makes a demand, neither a person, nor an idea, nor a moral law. Yet we all conform as much or more than people in an intensely authoritarian society would. Indeed, nobody is an authority except "It." What is It? Profit, economic necessities, the market, common sense, public opinion, what "one" does, thinks, feels. The laws of anonymous authority are as invisible as the laws of the market—and just as unassailable. Who can attack the invisible? Who can rebel against Nobody?[26]

By way of sympathetic rebuttal to Fromm, it should be pointed out that a sick society, one that violates the needs of men, will create its own peculiar forms of rebellion. Fromm would no doubt agree that an unhealthy body is the most likely harbor for a cancer. In this case it is the cancer of neurosis, mental illness, and random violence.

The important "Midtown Manhattan Study" is a case in point.[27] The study attempted not only to survey the incidence of mental impairment of the population of midtown Manhattan but also to inquire as to the economic correlates of mental health. The results were illuminating. 17.5 percent of the highest economic group was mentally impaired while 32.7 percent of the lowest economic group fitted the category. As far as the researchers could discern, only 23 percent of the highest class was mentally healthy, as was 9 percent of the lowest group.

When one notes that those in between were categorized by the researchers as neurotics, still barely able to function, the impact is devastating. The wealthy, even with their mobility and insulation from the chaos outside their homes, were able to produce barely one healthy individual out of four. The poorest, immersed in all of the urban malaise, unable to fend off the endemic corruptions of their environment, produced one healthy person out of ten. Fully one out of three of the poor could be labeled medically as psychotic.

    [26] Erich Fromm, *The Sane Society* (New York: Holt, Rinehart & Winston, Inc., 1955), pp. 152-153.
    [27] Leo Srole, Thomas Langner, et al., *The Midtown Manhattan Study: Mental Health in the Metropolis* (New York: McGraw Hill Book Company, 1962). The study excluded nonwhites.

It is true that this was an academic investigation. But when one examines the increasing tempo of violence and criminality in our cities, the assassinations, the riots and killings of 1966-69 which involved a score of urban centers, all very similar in environmental character to the mid-Manhattan of the poor, it is clear that the issue is a real one. Though the highest incidence of social disintegration can be found among our Negro poor in the cities, it ought not be concluded that these riotous actions constitute a lashing out at a racially exploitive society. The rural Negro of the South was at least as exploited as his urban descendants. Prejudice and lack of opportunity have had much to do in exacerbating the problem. But, surely, it must be the special, psychosocial conditions of our cities in the mass society that have precipitated the violence.

The Political Dimension

The most serious offshoot of modern mass culture is the position of dominance attained by political power. The state has fallen heir to the vast technological powers of our time. The coming of the modern mass industrial society and the demise of traditional monarchical forms was accompanied by the slaughter on the battlefields of World War I. World War II saw the first great expression of the potential for horror, made possible by the modern industrial state, on an as yet inconceivable level. Here we witnessed the unique perverseness inherent in the internal breakdown of the state, now having enormous technological wherewithal at its command. The rise of totalitarian societies in Germany, Russia, Japan, and Italy signaled the arrival of a new set of social and political conditions. The depredations of both fascism and communism against humanity surpassed in barbarism the most pessimistic prognosis of the future of civilized societies. The question has often been asked, How does one explain the actions of the German people, for example, in the light of their earlier achievements in education and culture?

An interesting and important hypothesis is set forth by Robert Nisbet in his book, *Community and Power.*[28] Nisbet points to the national state as the institutional form that pre-

[28] Robert Nisbet, *Community and Power* (New York: Oxford University Press, 1962).

cipitated totalitarianism. This position is somewhat different from E. H. Carr's view of the state as the protector of human rights as against the economic depredations of laissez-faire capitalism. Nisbet argues that the national state developed in the seventeenth and eighteenth centuries as an intellectual and social vehicle of modernity. During this period, with the aid of an assortment of philosophers and entrepreneurs, the state waged a continuing and ultimately successful struggle against the traditional authority structure, which had its roots in the Middle Ages—the manor, church, guild, town, and family.

In the name of progress, science, capitalism, free thought, and social mobility, the organic unity in diversity of the older institutional structures was gradually dissolved and in its stead a more qualitatively uniform and pervasive source of moral authority was born. From Hobbes and Rousseau to Hegel and Marx the state was offered as a higher unity binding together the multitudinous social atoms—the individual human beings. The coming of the totalitarian society, now representing the general will of its individual citizens rather than the varied and semiautonomous communities of the past, was ineluctable.

Nisbet argues that without the traditional intermediate allegiances of communities existing somewhat independent from each other, man has become defenseless; he has been caught in an extreme polarization between individual and society in which there exists no parity of power or compulsion. It is no wonder that Carr's rational elite, manipulating the mass irrationally, can be so easily transformed into an irrational elite. That this occurred practically simultaneously in a number of societies in our time testifies to the pervasive and possibly deterministic character of these social and political trends. The manipulators of this power now had unlimited capacity to shape the minds of men into an acceptance of the most bizarre and hallucinatory myths. Only since the mass society had reason itself become subject to the manipulations of the few in control of education and communication.

More striking is the evidence presented by Ernst Cassirer in *The Myth of the State*, in which the Nazi episode is related to the malfunctioning of the mass society.[29] Cassirer stated that

[29] Ernst Cassirer, *The Myth of the State* (Garden City, New York: Doubleday & Company, Inc., 1955).

the mass society, because of its centralized and interdependent structure, creates far more devastation if it falters than did earlier societies of greater diversity. The series of shocks and dislocations that culminated in the depression of the 1930's so confused the German people that they were susceptible to the most malignant mythology ever inflicted upon a civilized people. The ineffectuality of reason at the apex of the political hierarchy and the supine abdication of the educational system at the base of society, finally resulted in the seduction and surrender of both reason and will in the German people.

Instead of engaging in actions based upon a judicious assessment of experience, they were enveloped by a mythology that preyed upon their fears and anxieties, rooted as these were in the personal insecurity and aloneness imposed by the vast, impersonal industrial system. So eroded was their confidence in the autonomy of individual experience that all their traditional moral sense stood for nil. In its stead was manifested the most extreme depravity we have yet known. These acts were actually committed by a significant portion of the population and buttressed by a moral apathy and disinterest on the part of the rest:

> Methods of compulsion and suppression have ever been used in political life. But in most cases these methods aimed at material results. Even the most fearful systems of despotism contented themselves with forcing upon men certain laws of action. They were not concerned with the feeling, judgements, and thoughts of men. It is true that in the great religious struggles the most violent efforts were made not only to rule the actions of men but also their consciousness. But these attempts were bound to fail; they only strengthened the feeling for religious liberty. Now the modern political myths proceeded in quite a different manner. They did not begin with demanding or prohibiting certain actions. They undertook to change the men, in order to be able to regulate and control their deeds. The political myths acted in the same way as a serpent that tries to paralyze its victims before attacking them. Men fell victims without any serious resistance. They were vanquished and subdued before they had realized what actually happened.
>
> The usual means of political oppression would not have sufficed to produce this effect. Even under the hardest political pressure men have not ceased living their own lives. There has always remained a sphere of personal freedom resistant to this pressure. The classical ethical ideas of antiquity maintained and

strengthened their force amidst the chaos and the political decay
of the ancient world. . . . Our modern political myths destroyed
all those ideas and ideals before they began to work. They do not
have to fear any opposition from this quarter. . . . The myth of
the race worked like a strong corrosive and succeeded in dissolv-
ing and disintegrating all other values.[30]

The patterns and problems of the mass society are part of a
trend that has existed in the world for generations. The gross
events we have seen take place in a world so full of self-pride
have not been anachronistic accidents. They are part of an
endemic flaw in social structure that we have inherited. What
we have seen in the way of human perversity will not be the last
of these trends. Indeed, it can happen here. The question remains: What is the meaning of what has happened?

If we follow the suggestions of Carr and Nisbet, the movement toward modernity would be interpreted as having as its
theme the liberation from a past of inequality and want in favor
of economic sufficiency and technological advance. The dominance of the national state is unthinkable unless one includes
the concomitant surge of industrial development of the late
eighteenth and early nineteenth century. Such power was too
much for any of the old institutions to come to terms with. The
unifications in society, the interdependence of mankind in
space and time could be accomplished only through a source of
authority that would transcend all the old divisions.

The state fulfilled a special heuristic function. It made
things work in terms of all the people. And as the nineteenth
century advanced into the twentieth the quantities of people
increased astronomically; the state should have become relatively more efficient. To be sure, there were material advances.
Yet the conditions of life in the urban centers became worse
than anything the rural areas could match. The masses still
persisted. Their collective acquiescence in misery implicitly reflected an acceptance of technological priorities and political
centralism.

The Role of Science and Technology

The role of science was as important as were economics and
the state in furthering this state of affairs. Even before indus-

[30] Cassirer, *op. cit.*, pp. 360-361.

trialism, scientific thought had had its impact on the intellectual world, in philosophy, politics, and economics. Galileo's vision of a universe of matter in motion and Newton's subsequent great synthesis were soon utilized to speed the development of the industrial and technological revolution. Man thus committed himself to a belief in the reality and primacy of the material world and of the universal system of scientific laws that explained it. Science has since become a marvelous and sometimes esoteric alchemy for stripping away the secrets of nature. Once uncovered this knowledge of reality can inevitably be put to man's use through the powers of technology.

The fact that we are in tune with these external material forces is thus supposedly evidenced by the great industrial and technological success elicited by science, now possible for all men. Man has been freed of his historic enslavement to brute labor. That this success has been gained at a price and that new forms of enslavement have been precipitated is not recognized by a populace who define slavery to fit their own swollen sense of achievement. Victory over many traditional natural foes of man—hunger, pestilence, and the varied forms of social impoverization—is argument enough for the view that matter is central, that these natural forces are to be obeyed rather than controlled or even thwarted. The social system that best exploits these capacities in man and nature is the appropriate one. And today that system seems to be the great national state.

The change in our social structure from a society predominantly agricultural to a nation of large urban centers, with all its accompanying upsets in the balance between man and nature, has been tacitly accepted by our populace, not necessarily because of the intrinsic benefits of megalopolis but because of the belief that these complexes are natural and necessary for the support of our industrial enterprises. Without the urban society, presumably man would not be able to produce those artifacts of material existence necessary to our population. The fact that many people escape the central city for the suburbs is, on the other hand, testimony to a different set of desires on the part of man. In this special circumstance, the two needs, those of the organized industrial society and those of human sensitivity, are harmonized through a barely adequate transportation system.

There are other outcomes of the mass society's acceptance

of this philosophy of realistic materialism. As Carr has shown, the individualistic laissez-faire society of the eighteenth and nineteenth centuries was inherently unstable. The social and economic dislocation that resulted from vicious competition in the marketplace inevitably brought about private monopolies and usually governmental intervention. The locus of control over society was increasingly centralized. In the name of efficiency, once the lines of interdependence were clearly established in the society, controls over the entire apparatus became a necessity. Individual autonomy, local control, and a host of auxiliary values were soon eliminated because of this supposed need for efficiency.

Today we are in the midst of a continuing technological revolution. Our belief in the omnipotence of the historic drive to acquire greater material control over our environment and our dependence upon the continued unfolding of this chain of events for the welfare of man have caught us in an intellectual vise. It is conceivable that, even if there were evidence to prove the economic and social inefficiency of the existing organizational edifices, we would ignore it, so committed are we to the institutional framework of the mass society. Witness our recent precipitous growth in population. Seemingly, our situation may demand insuperable achievements in social engineering to turn us onto another historical road.

> Before man can transcend himself he is being dehumanized. Before he can elevate his mind, it is being deadened. Freedom is placed before him and snatched away. The rich and varied life he might lead is standardized. This breeds anxiety, and the vicious circle begins anew, for as we are objects of manipulation, our anxiety is exploitable. The mass grows; we are more alike than ever; and feel a deeper sense of entrapment and loneliness. And even if the incubus of hydrogen war could be lifted, these spectors would still hover over us.[31]

Perhaps the situation is not quite as bad as this. But it ought to be better.

EDUCATIONAL PROBLEMS

The question next arises, How does this new set of social circumstances affect our educational system. Here is where the

[31] Bernard Rosenberg, *Mass Culture, op. cit.*, p. 9.

altruism and vision of all people is concentrated. For in directing the young toward the ideals and dreams that have evaded
the older generation, there has always been hope and redemption. One would think that in our schools the purposes and
content of learning would be intrinsic. Here we could find an
oasis of truth where the cash value of an idea would never be
raised.

Yet in more terrible days, pictures of Hitler depicted
him parading through fields of daises, surrounded by cherubic,
blond German children, children who at that time were receiving the warm educational succoring, the *Gemütlichkeit* for
which the Germans were so famous. The love of children, the
kindness and gentleness children are exposed to in their early
years is thus no sure guide to the consequent shaping of their
destinies.

And it is true that in our own time, our enlightened schools
and leadership have meekly accepted the patterns and priorities
of the dominant social forces. It is helpful to recall earlier eras
of educational preoccupations and educational leaders such as
Horace Mann, Thaddeus Stevens, William Torrey Harris, Francis
Parker, John Dewey, and William H. Kilpatrick. Each of these
thinkers and educators stood for a peculiarly American kind of
idealism as well as intellectual realism. The essential purpose of
education to these men was not the meeting of the immediate
practical needs of society, but the long-range creation of an
enlightened democracy. The shift in our perspectives on education can be discerned by referring to those who now exert
leadership, who have given us the most recent impetus for
reform.

It is only a few years since the names of Hyman Rickover,
James Conant, and Myron Lieberman were preeminent among a
series of critics attempting to get American education onto the
high road of accommodation with the urgent requirements of
modern American society.[32] The major concerns of their vari-

---

[32] Hyman G. Rickover, *Education and Freedom* (New York: Dutton
& Co., Inc., 1957); James Conant, *Slums and Suburbs* (New York,
McGraw-Hill Book Company, 1961) and *The Education of American
Teachers* (New York, McGraw-Hill Book Company, 1963); Myron
Lieberman, *Education as a Profession* (Englewood Cliffs, N.J.: Prentice-
Hall, Inc., 1956) and *The Future of Public Education* (Chicago: University
of Chicago Press, 1960).

ous statements were: control of teacher education, size of high schools, the state of mathematics, science, and foreign language curricula, elite federal schools, teachers organizations versus unions, education as a weapon of national defense.

All of these issues in some way reflect what was and is happening in our society. They demonstrate again the manner in which educational institutions have followed current social trends. They have given automatic assent to what is going on outside the halls of ivy—because of the need for institutional survival. Occasionally this is rationalized in terms of service to the community. The line between service and absorption and identification becomes increasingly attenuated. These responses have grown out of and are congruent with the evolving character of our organized, mass technological society. The deeper, philosophical involvements of education with substantive, alternative values have been bypassed. Indeed, Lieberman has explicitly stated these philosophical problems to be of no special concern to educators, since supposedly there are no controversies concerning education that arise from differing philosophical positions.[33]

The implicit assumption here is that all is well with our society and that the great need is to make our education imitate the maximum efficiency of our technological institutions and to produce individuals who will easily fit and bolster the values of these institutions. In a sense, we have the modern counterpart of that situation described by Raymond Callahan in *Education and the Cult of Efficiency*, in which early twentieth-century educators attempted to shape the public educational system in the image of the large-scale business enterprises of that era.[34] Just as the mentality of the efficiency expert dominated that era, so do many current managers of the educational system think in terms of the manipulation of the externals of the enterprise and not of the rationale for the educational venture. Note the educational values of Clark Kerr in his discussion of the ends of the "multiversity" at a time when as President of the University of California, he represented the most advanced

[33] Myron Lieberman, *The Future of Public Education*, p. 15.
[34] Raymond Callahan, *Education and the Cult of Efficiency* (Chicago: University of Chicago Press, 1962).

views of the function of higher education:

> Knowledge has certainly never in history been so central to the conduct of an entire society. What the railroads did for the second half of the nineteenth century and the automobile for the first half of this century, the knowledge industry may do for the second half of this century: that is, to serve as the focal point for national growth. And the university is at the center of the knowledge process.[35]

Edgar Friedenberg has commented that the vision of the city of intellect that Kerr saw from his vantage point as creator of the multiversity looks oddly like downtown Los Angeles.

The persuasiveness of the corporate image of life has already extended itself to the philosophers of education. In *Education and the New America*, two educational theorists recommend that we drop the image of an individualistic America and conform to the needs of the corporate society.[36] Let us attempt to create a climate of freedom within the system, they argue, by cultivating democratic processes and scientific rationality within that society and its schools. The authors do note that the inner workings of the corporation are inevitably hierarchical and autocratic for the sake of expediting decision making. But they do not ask whether democracy and scientific rationality can be realized when we make a commitment to a basically irrational and enslaving system of social values.

There are, to be true, more insightful thinkers, such as Edgar Friedenberg and Paul Goodman, who see the shallowness of our educational tampering.[37] They see clearly that it is the massiveness and externality of our social institutions that lead to our children's lack of interest in education and that juvenile delinquency is reflective of the void created by a system in which genuine labor has no place and work is created from the

---

[35] Clark Kerr, *The Uses of the University* (Cambridge, Mass.: Harvard University Press, 1963).

[36] Solon Kimball and James McClellan, *Education and the New America* (New York: Random House, Inc., 1962).

[37] Edgar Friedenberg, *The Vanishing Adolescent* (New York: Dell Publishing, Co., 1959) and *Coming of Age in America* (New York: Dell Publishing, Co., 1965); Paul Goodman, *Growing Up Absurd* (New York: Random House, Inc., 1960), *Compulsory Miseducation* and *The Community of Scholars* (New York: Random House, Inc., 1963).

symbols of a paper economy, meaningless outside of its own self-perpetuation.[38]

For the most part, those who are listened to in education today are attuned to the more persuasive attitudes in our society—bigness and economic efficiency. The themes of Conant, Lieberman, Kerr, and Rickover, while divergent on many points of method and control, all converge when these larger ideas are enunciated. The need for a national system of education, an ever larger structure having uniform criteria and controls, seems fundamental to all their assumptions and expectations concerning the future of education. They find the traditional local orientation of education to be anachronistic in our time. Like the national communications media, a uniform educational system must reach into every corner of our society to achieve an evenness of achievement and thus eventually a similarity of vision and understanding.[39]

CONCLUSION

The system is pervasive but not impregnable. It carried within it the seeds of its ultimate dissolution. Yet there is no way of insuring that what follows will be any better. Our argument is that one trend in human thought and action has been preempted as exhausting all the possibilities for social arrangements in culture. It has resulted in the reification of bigness, centralization, and impersonality in all our institutions. The acceptance by the masses of this implicit philosophy has resulted in the inundation of the individual in an environment over which he has no control. "All he can do is to fall into step like a marching soldier or a worker on the endless belt. He can act; but the sense of independence, significance is gone.[40]

There are other alternatives consistent with the good of man. We may yet find a way to nurture those quiet virtues of the communal life, so natural to man at one time, yet today so

[38] David Bazelon, *The Paper Economy* (New York: Random House, Inc., 1963).

[39] See the technocratic orientation of Francis Keppel, *The Necessary Revolution in American Education* (New York: Harper & Row, Publishers, 1966).

[40] Erich Fromm, *Escape from Freedom* (New York: Farrar, Rinehart & Co., 1941), p. 132.

"irrational" because they seem not to fit the corporate society image. The idea that there can be a place for individualism in a living community has to be defended.[41] Too often man is made to feel that the only way he can exhibit his individuality is to resign from the "organized system," to give up those prized securities and material advantages modern life has given him, become a hippie, a yippie, or an outcast on the Bowery.[42] The individual who can find nourishment in a unique cultural purview of life is rare. The mass society cannot tolerate the existence of pluralities or of humans sharing deep and differing values and cultural concerns, whether they be religious, ethnic, intellectual, or artistic. Shut off from developing pathways of communication to the larger public, from associating through cultural transactions with the outside world for fear of being absorbed into the corporate system as most of them eventually are, the small enclaves of pluralism have become increasingly bizarre. They have become fixed in their historical evolution to the only image of themselves that infuses their culture with a sense of social reality—the past.[43]

The need then is for a philosophical counterattack upon the implicit assumptions that have led to our current social situation and in the case of our special professional concern, the inevitable intellectual sterilization of our educational system. We cannot hope to counter the powerful thrust of the present value system of massiveness except by presenting philosophical alternatives. As pluralistic cultural differences in our society are gradually eliminated, it will become more difficult to persuade people to value what they do not have and thus cannot know. But while there are still a few lively centers of divergent cultural values cherished by significant segments of our population, there will be an experiential basis for men to realize real and meaningful alternatives to this massive and monolithic society. To do this we first need to reexamine some of the classical if recent American views on the nature of the democratic social life.

[41] Alan Wheelis, *The Quest for Identity* (New York: W. W. Norton & Company, Inc., 1958).

[42] Paul Goodman, *Growing Up Absurd* (New York: Random House, Inc., 1960).

[43] Examples of this can be found in the Amish, Hutterite, and Hassidic religious sects.

chapter 2

Dewey and Cultural Pluralism

Our historical experience has been unique in that Americans have never had to confront the issue of cultural pluralism directly, with the exception of a short but significant period at the end of the nineteenth and the beginning of the twentieth century. The expanding frontiers, the vast underdeveloped areas that served to extinguish differences through the common challenges that transcended cultures, allowed us to bypass the philosophical and social issues involved.

Today the confrontation cannot be avoided. If we are to rescue ourselves from the dehumanization that has resulted from the structure of the mass society, we must discover for ourselves and delineate an entirely new set of choices and freedoms. While the philosophical basis for pluralism must, like the social context, be considered anew, it is important that we examine the past to understand the nature of prior failures and so perhaps mitigate future errors. Also, it is important to note the intellectual context that allowed the progressive philosophers of the early twentieth century to postulate a pluralistic vision of American culture and democracy that was substantive—that is, not so much framed in material and institutional terms as directed toward building a society that could allow each individual to achieve the good life.

The philosophy of cultural pluralism as proposed by Dewey and the various progressives of the early decades of the twentieth century failed to find a place within our culture. To a large extent, the swift passage of historic events played the major role in dissipating support for this position. In many ways the manner in which the pluralistic vision was disregarded by those in authority substantiated Dewey's prognostications that the path our nation was following could ultimately lead to the violation of our democratic creed.

The failure of the philosophy of pluralism derives from more than the accidents of history or the conscious rejection of our leadership; there was also a failure in the intellectual realm. The philosophical arguments adduced in favor of pluralism contained significant gaps and thus did not evoke a response in the general perception of human experience that could have stemmed the process of assimilation.

We shall examine Dewey's philosophy in the context of its relation to the movement of cultural pluralism. Dewey's views constitute one of the most important philosophical contributions to the definition of the democratic life in terms of its sources in basic conceptions of man, nature, and experience. We shall also examine the varied responses of men such as Horace Kallen and I. B. Berkson, whose philosophies were deeply influenced by Dewey. Both Kallen and Berkson came to differing positions on the nature and extent of pluralism in our society. In so doing they testify implicitly to certain ambiguities in Dewey's instrumentalism that give cause for the eventual intellectual debilitation of cultural pluralism on the American scene.

JOHN DEWEY'S PHILOSOPHY

Personal Influence in Dewey's Philosophy

Dewey often stated that an understanding of his philosophy necessitated an understanding of the background, experiences, and values that made him the person he was.[1] Born in Burlington, Vermont in 1859 (the year of Darwin's *Origin of the Species*) of middle-class parents, Dewey was perhaps the most typically American of all our philosophers. The New England small-town democracy was certainly important in giving him that perennial optimistic expectancy concerning the efficacy of human intelligence and the sense of possibility that American democracy contained. This strong faith in reason might also have derived from a transmutation of the New Englander's tra-

---

[1] Gail Kennedy, "John Dewey," in Max Fisch (ed.), *Classic American Philosophers* (New York: Appleton-Century-Crofts, 1951), p. 329.

ditionally deep religious commitment to a more secular social context.

As Dewey progressed from the status of student to teacher, he became aware of the importance of education in widening those common-sense experiences that came from his personal environment into a more intellectually abstract and universal position. His commitment to philosophy was a natural outgrowth of the interaction of his special personal genius and his background. Even his early Hegelian philosophical commitment was a typically Americanized version of the European forms. Embodied in this liberal Hegelianism as a central tenet was the belief in the need for social unification in our society, in which each individual participated and was incorporated in the larger organic totality of things.[2]

His experiences in the Midwest as a professor of philosophy were heightened in these respects by the informality of the society of these rural areas.[3] Men met together in these communities, as they did in New England, to solve the issues that lay before them. Here, more so even than in New England, an unencumbered intellectual pragmatism allowed the settler great freedom in his choice of alternate solutions, depending upon the particular practical circumstances.

In 1890 a copy of William James' *Principles of Psychology* came into Dewey's hands. The arguments of this philosopher-psychologist concerning the nature of human behavior and its biological causes were extremely persuasive.[4] To see human functioning in terms of the satisfaction of the practical and natural ends of the species seemed to confirm intellectually what Dewey saw happening in life around him. The Darwinian outlook of James' psychology set off a resonant response in Dewey's writings.[5] Man must be conceived of as a biological creature, a product of the natural fires of evolution. In order to understand the ways in which human beings respond to their

[2] Gail Kennedy, *op. cit.* On pages 331-332 Kennedy cites Dewey's early *Psychology* (New York: Appleton-Century-Crofts, 1887) as an example of this quality in his thought.
[3] At University of Michigan (1884-1889, 1890-1894), University of Minnesota (1889-1890).
[4] Kennedy, p. 332.
[5] See for example *The Influence of Darwinism on Philosophy* (New York: Henry Holt and Co., 1910).

environment and act out their experiences in life, Dewey maintained that we ought to realize that all actions are predicated on the satisfaction of human needs. Men will alter their behavior until they have realized a dynamic stability with their environment in a world that is constantly evolving and changing. The test of the validity of any activity and its intellectual rationale is the success with which it allows the organism to function. Human behavior and intelligence, too, according to Dewey, are instrumental in intent, aiming at the satisfaction of the practical demands of life.[6]

When Dewey moved to Chicago in 1894 he entered an urban environment in which a new dimension to the American experience was being created. Here rural America was being transformed into a vast urban industrial society. The clear-cut environmental challenges and dangers that men had to face in the rural context were considerably altered in the context of the late nineteenth-century metropolis. Survival was conceived not in terms of natural challenges but rather in social terms. The biological jungle became an asphalt jungle.

Dewey saw immediately that the traditional solutions to the American way worked out in the agrarian environment would not work in the city. The new problems were created by man. They were dynamic and complex, not amenable to a simple examination of alternatives that could be made and tested by citizens of the small towns. A new interpretation of the use of man's natural faculties became necessary in this context.[7] It was here that the importance of science, so clearly demonstrated in the intellectual revolution that Darwin had stimulated, could be seen. These attitudes of mind had also created the technological revolution so visible in the cities. It was now necessary to apply the methods of science in the area of man's social life to ameliorate the frenzied dislocations and sufferings induced by that same revolution science had created.

In addition, it was apparent that the individualistic rural virtues implicit in the lives of small-town America had to be clarified. In a society going through a drastic social change, what heretofore existed as an informally accepted set of values

---

[6] Gail Kennedy, *op. cit.*, p. 333.
[7] See Dewey's educational formulation of this issue in *School and Society* (Chicago: University of Chicago Press, 1956), p. 9.

for human existence had to be reinterpreted, formalized, and rooted in a philosophy of human nature. Here Dewey's natural acceptance of individual experience was transformed into a quasi-metaphysical virtue. The individual's experience must be brought to the center of the new intellectual and social stage.[8]

It was in Chicago that all these strands began to come together, both philosophically and practically. Not long after Dewey became head of the departments of philosophy, psychology, and pedagogy, at the University of Chicago, he instituted the famous laboratory school where he attempted to give substance to his views on human nature, intelligence, and experience. Dewey felt the school was the institution specially fitted for the role of developing the scientific rationality latent in the individual that could, when developed, capacitate him for living in the complex mobility of an ever-changing society.[9]

Human Nature

Although it was not until much later (in *Human Nature and Conduct*) that Dewey explicitly elaborated the logic of his views toward human nature and society, his philosophy was being acted out in the laboratory school, at least until he left Chicago in 1904. The strength of these practical views on democracy and education ultimately lay in the richer philosophical basis given them later.

Dewey had always postulated the biological factor as being basic to human activity. He labeled it "impulse." But this driving organic impetus was not the rigidly directed drives of lower animal forms.[10] Men's instinctual equipment was considerably attenuated in his evolutionary development from the simian level. As early as 1896, in an article entitled "The Reflex Arc Concept in Psychology," Dewey expressed this liberation from the simplistic behavioral models that attempted to reduce human actions to the patterns of organic adaptation.[11]   Later he

[8] John Dewey, *Experience and Nature* (New York: W. W. Norton & Company, Inc., 1958), pp. 242-247.
[9] See his *School and Society* (Chicago: University of Chicago Press, 1956), p. 12.
[10] John Dewey, *Human Nature and Conduct* (New York: Henry Holt and Co., 1922), p. 95ff.
[11] Wayne Dennis (ed.), *Readings in the History of Psychology* (New York: Appleton-Century-Crofts, 1948).

would deny that human instincts could be compared with animal patterns of behavior. The latter are always directed toward specific goals. In man, they show no such specificity.[12]

Perhaps the most positive aspect of this basic biological residuum for the individual and ultimately for society lies in the fact that impulse is the source of all individuality and innovation. It is a constant reservoir of novelty, which cannot be turned aside, for it is reborn in each human being striving to direct the novel organic patterns of life into a world constantly in flux.[13] But as Dewey noted, undirected and unchannelled, this energy breeds anarchy and chaos. Impulse does not have instinctual specificity and unless it is directed into socially ordered pathways it becomes a source of dislocation for individual and community.

So is born the need for a more conserving factor in human nature—the institutions of society. Society represents those habitual patterns of activity that give rhythm and continuity to human existence. Here, the vitality of impulse can be guided into ordered forms of behavior and given meaning. Through social habits and institutions, the impulses of man can be structured so as to insure the growth of individuality within its only possible context, culture. The individual can thus be provided with a frame within which his own unique potentialities, rooted in the special interactions of biological and social factors, can be realized.

On a larger scale, one may note that the impulses of men, concentrated as they are in social unities, have a way of giving a unique quality to each society. Here, Dewey elaborated on the purely social qualities of the problem of human individuality. He felt it was the habitual institutional patterns that had the power to stimulate or thwart the individual in the realization of his special individuality.

> In fact only in a society dominated by modes of belief and admiration fixed by past custom is habit any more conservative than it is progressive. It all depends upon its quality. Habit is an ability, an art, formed through past experience. But whether an ability is limited to repetition of past acts adapted to past

[12] John Dewey, *Human Nature and Conduct, op. cit.*, p. 105.
[13] Dewey, *ibid.*, p. 95.

conditions or is available for new emergencies depends wholly upon what kind of habit exists.[14]

Historically, societies have reflected the tensions between individual impulse and social institutions. The biological impulsive factor has been constant. It is one with the species. The responsibility for the mode of resolving this tension has devolved upon society. It is in the character of cultures that we find the clue to these traditional difficulties. Dewey noted that societies have fluctuated between those having uncoordinated, and thus anarchic institutions and those whose structures have been so encrusted as to allow no possibility for change. Of the two extremes, he felt the latter to be a more pervasive condition of society.

The result of the traditionally repressive organization of society has been the constant and unremitting war between the individual and society. And while the drives of innovation may be thwarted by the resisting forms of society, in the end the expansive energies of man are realized, if only to break out of the rigid, recalcitrant, and uncreative institutional structure of society:

> The place of impulse in conduct as a pivot of re-adjustment, re-organization, in habits may be defined as follows: On one side, it is marked off from the territory of arrested and encrusted habits. On the other side, it is demarcated from the region in which impulse is a law unto itself.* Generalizing these distinctions, a valid moral theory contrasts with all those theories which set up static goals (even when they are called perfection), and with those theories which idealize raw impulse and find in its spontaneities an adequate mode of human freedom. Impulse is a source, an indispensable source, of liberation; but only as it is employed in giving habits pertinence and freshness does it liberate power.
>
> *[Dewey's footnote] The use of the words instinct and impulse as practical equivalents is intentional, even though it may grieve critical readers. The word instinct taken alone is still too laden with the older notion that an instinct is always definitely organized and adapted—which for the most part is just what it is not in human beings. The word impulse suggests something primitive, yet loose, undirected, initial. Man can progress as beasts cannot, precisely because he has so many "instincts" that they cut across one another, so that most serviceable actions must be

[14] Dewey, *ibid.*, p. 66.

learned. In learning habits it is possible for man to learn the habit of learning. Then betterment becomes a conscious principle of life.[15]

The historical record produced by this clash between two basic human needs is available for all to see. It is a history of wars, persecutions, revolutions, hatred, prejudice, and exploitation. It was, it is true, punctuated by eras of peace in which men were able to express in their cultural existence some of the more sublime attributes of human nature. By and large, the tragedy of human existence has been underscored by man's inability to hold in balance these polar capacities.

This inability was diagnosed by Dewey to be caused by a retarded development of man's innate faculties for dealing rationally with his circumstances. Dewey was rationalist enough to see that man's biological and social nature includes that unique capacity of reason that separates man from more primitive forms of life. In keeping with his valuing of experimental intelligence, Dewey proposed that the scientific method was what was needed to eradicate the shibboleths and dogmas of outworn intellectual forms that have fixed man to outmoded institutional patterns of life.[16]

Experience is the test of every form of social existence. If it allows each person to utilize his unique capacities, then the social forms are valid. If, on the other hand, social institutions give rise to dislocations and tensions—if they do not change to meet the new challenges of time itself—then we must be prepared for periodic disasters. Scientific intelligence becomes the key to resolving the dilemmas inevitably confronting an ever-changing experiential context.

Education is crucial, because in it lies the opportunity to effect those changes of attitude and behavior through which a rational society might be created. Dewey's concentration on the school as the instrument for rationalizing society was a necessary outgrowth of his philosophy. First of all, Dewey had come out of a milieu that was education-conscious. His earliest professional work was as a school teacher. Second, and perhaps most important, was the historic role that Dewey felt public education has had in our society.

[15] Dewey, *ibid.*, pp. 104-105.
[16] *Ibid.*, p. 172.

Since the beginning of the Common School movement, public education has always been linked with the ideal of uplifting the masses of the people so they may take their rightful place in our society. The dream of an enlightened polity, as early exemplified in the writings of Horace Mann, has always been a force behind the spread and the strengthening of the public school. At the time he was formulating his views, Dewey was able to relate his purely philosophical insights to the practical opportunities presented by the University of Chicago Laboratory School. The school was to be a microcosm of a universal endeavor to build into the child's development a respect for his natural inclinations. This respect was to be centered around the child's natural sense of judicious experimentation, which, given a high degree of cultivation, could breed out the susceptibility to unreason and social irresponsibility that had been for so long a seemingly integral aspect of human behavior.[17]

View of Democracy

The scientific, experimental attitude was the means to achieve the highest value that could come out of the cultivation of intelligence in human nature. This highest value was what Dewey called "democracy." This was perhaps a special use of the term democracy, especially considering its usual connotations. Dewey did not mean to describe any special political, constitutional, or legal condition of life. Nor did democracy in its broader, philosophical use encompass the social and economic extensions of the term, which, even at the turn of the century, were effecting important changes in our social structure: "A democracy is more than a form of government, it is primarily a mode of associated living, of conjoint communicated experience."[18]

Dewey meant democracy to describe a broad experiential condition under which men could live. The democratic society is a society in which each individual is able, through the freely capacitated use of his faculties, to fulfill his potentialities.[19]

[17] John Dewey, *The Child and the Curriculum* (Chicago: University of Chicago Press, 1956), pp. 17-22, and *Democracy and Education* (New York: Macmillan Company, 1916), pp. 224-226.

[18] John Dewey, *Democracy and Education*, p. 101.

[19] *Ibid.*, p. 101.

This takes place when the society commits all of its attention to the use of scientific intelligence in adjusting the structure and function of its institutions to meet the changing circumstances of history. The true democracy is never this particular economic or political form or that particular social or religious set of values.[20] The truth of any special institutional envisagement in society is predicated on its workability, i.e., on its ability to meet both the total needs of society and the special and particular demands made by each individual in realizing his freedoms and his potentialities.

If Dewey believed in any one permanent and enduring if not absolute value, it was in scientific reasoning. To him it was the paradigm of human intelligence and an instrumentality for ascertaining the pragmatic utility of any social commitment. Scientific method is the most highly developed method of confronting experience critically. Man has been engaged in this process of critical reexamination continuously since the beginning of culture.

The gradual development of man's rational abilities has now, in the scientific method, brought us to the point where we can direct this critical capability to the eventual solution of our social problems. Through scientific intelligence we can now hope to release the capacities of each human being for a fruition limited only by the natural talents and inclinations of each person, rather than by the external accidents of birth, environment, or other irrelevant social considerations.

> I have emphasized in what precedes the importance of the effective release of intelligence in connection with personal experience in the democratic way of living. I have done so purposely because democracy is so often and so naturally associated in our minds with freedom of *action*, forgetting the importance of freed intelligence which is necessary to direct and to warrant freedom of action. Unless freedom of individual action has intelligence and informed conviction back of it, its manifestation is almost sure to result in confusion and disorder. The democratic idea of freedom is not the right of each individual to *do* as he pleases, even if it be qualified by adding "provided he does not interfere with the same freedom on the part of others." While the idea is not always, or not often enough, expressed in words, the

---

[20] "Democracy and Educational Administration," *School and Society*, (April 1937), reprinted in Joseph Ratner (ed.), *Intelligence in the Modern World* (New York: Random House, Inc., 1939), p. 400.

basic freedom is that of freedom of *mind* and of whatever degree
of freedom of action and experience is necessary to produce freedom of intelligence. The modes of freedom guaranteed in the Bill
of Rights are all of this nature: Freedom of belief and conscience,
of expression of opinion, of assembly for discussion and conference, of the press as an organ of communication. They are guaranteed because without them individuals are not free to develop
and society is deprived of what they might contribute.[21]

The Social Context

Dewey always intended that his analysis of human nature
and scientific thought be a prolegomenon to an analysis of the
existing state of things in society. The entire focus of his philosophical undertaking was toward the amelioration of conditions
that hindered the free expression of individuality. Thus he felt
it was crucial that he examine society to locate those social
areas needing the clear light of scientific rationality.[22]

Almost seventy years ago Dewey saw the great problem that
confronted our society and that stood in the way of the realization of its democratic vision. He felt it was our massive industrialization. It was evident to him that Chicago at the turn of
the century was the prototype of things to come.[23] And on
coming to New York a few years later, he saw only more evidence to support his original convictions. The massive, externalized anonymity spawned by the industrialized society was even
then a fact. Men fitted into the demands of the machine. It was
a society in which an individual had little more responsibility to
his community than to appear regularly at the factory gate and
engage in his monotonous routine for his appointed time. On
returning home, he entered an apartment or tenement house,
knowing few of his neighbors, having few interests in them or in
his locality. He was an anonymous, alienated, undeveloped organism.[24]

In Dewey's writings on social philosophy, this concern became a dominant theme.[25] He saw the disappearance of the

[21] Dewey, "Intelligence," in Joseph Ratner (ed.), *op. cit.* p. 404.
[22] Dewey, *Liberalism and Social Action* (New York: G. P. Putnam's
Sons, 1935), p. 44.
[23] Dewey, *School and Society* (Chicago: University of Chicago Press,
1956), pp. 23-24.
[24] Dewey, *Individualism Old and New* (New York: Minton Balch,
1930), pp. 51-73.
[25] See John Childs, *American Pragmatism and Education* (New York:
Holt, Rinehart & Winston, Inc., 1956).

original American social structure, through which scientific intelligence might have been disseminated. The smaller communities of America, within which the traditional religious and economic beliefs had been rooted, provided for Dewey the paradigmatic type of social structure that fitted his views of a democracy to serve human needs.[26] What was deficient in those communities was an awareness that the common sense pragmatism they demonstrated in their daily lives, especially in the light of the laissez-faire agrarian economics and the fundamentalist religious and philosophical beliefs, would eventually fail as an adaptive intellectual solution to the problems brought about by a world in a hectic state of flux. This was especially so when one considered that the changes were being brought about by new forms of technology and new patterns of life that flowed from this technology.[27]

In the urban areas, however, the new forms were causing even more dislocations in the traditional community structure. The philosophy of laissez-faire economics was being used to rationalize a social and economic system that was dislocating man from his traditional sources of community life and responsibility.[28] Dewey was concerned with this misguided and misconceived individualism that looked upon man as a freely precipitated atom, unconnected and unresponsive to the thoughts and needs of the larger society.[29]

To be meaningful, individuality had to be set within a community of other minds, where shared experiences could shape the innovating tendency in all men.

> From the standpoint of the individual, it [democracy] consists in having a responsible share according to capacity in forming and directing the activities of the groups to which one belongs and in participating according to need in the values which the groups sustain. From the standpoint of the groups, it demands liberation of the potentialities of members of a group in harmony with the interests and goods which are common. Since every individual is a member of many groups, this specification cannot

[26] Dewey, *Freedom and Culture* (New York: G. P. Putnam's Sons, 1939), pp. 50-73.
[27] *Ibid.*, pp. 70-73.
[28] Dewey, *Individualism Old and New* (New York: Minton Balch, 1930), pp. 65-69.
[29] Dewey, *The Public and Its Problems* (New York: Henry Holt and Co., 1927), pp. 156-157.

be fulfilled except when different groups interact flexibly and fully in connection with other groups.[30]

THE DEVELOPMENT OF CULTURAL PLURALISM

With each passing year Dewey's dream of a democracy that would mobilize the critical capacities of all men was undermined by the dynamics of the industrialized urban society. In a society in which the individual was a member of a mass, there could be little opportunity for his own voice to be heard. Through the use of the potent machinery of our mass-communications industry, men could be mesmerized to conform. Government could not be responsive to the voice of the people, because the existing publics had been dissolved into the mass. Increasingly irrational techniques had to be used to obtain conformity.

A society composed of interweaving publics able to generate large-scale intelligent confrontations of the problems of life could scarcely be expected under such conditions. And yet this expectation of a plural society made up of any number of self-regulating communities, all open to the larger world and taking part in a dialogue of shared intelligence with other communities, was a necessary conclusion of Dewey's conception of human nature and democracy.[31] Dewey's problem was to confront this conflict of theory and reality with a particular program of social reconstruction.

The Problem of Immigration

In this context Dewey became associated with a concerted intellectual attempt to provide a rationale for a pluralistic conception of democracy. Those in the forefront of the philosophy of cultural pluralism were not by chance students of Dewey. They were deeply influenced by him and thus committed to his larger philosophical and educational goals.

The pluralistic philosophy as it was proposed would supplement Dewey's vision of a democratic dialogue of communities committed to the improvement of society. Perhaps this quality

[30] *Ibid.*, p. 147.
[31] Dewey, *Democracy and Education* (New York: Macmillan Company, 1916), p. 102.

of supplementation in Dewey's use of cultural pluralism explains the weakness in the movement as well as the insufficiently detailed proposals in Dewey's general writings on social philosophy.

In the period between 1890 and 1920 occurred the largest influx of immigrants of non-Anglo-Saxon ethnic background in the history of our nation. The large numbers of these immigrants and their variance from the cultural norms of the resident majority caused tremendous social and intellectual ferment. How could this populace be digested and absorbed into our society?

America has always had a minority problem. The original colonies of the seventeenth century encompassed a variety of cultural and religious traditions. But under the English hegemony, which began in the late 1600's and continued into the eighteenth century, the English tradition became the dominant, even the orthodox version of America. By the revolutionary era this dominance was so ingrained that a staunch libertarian like Benjamin Franklin could concern himself about the Anglo-Norman homogeneity of our culture and propose to his state of Pennsylvania that it endeavor as a cardinal tenet of its yet unestablished educational system to educate the Pennsylvania Germans to the use of more acceptable English.

Thus very early it was assumed that the vast open spaces of America would provide the perfect setting for the blending of various traditions into a new American set of values, albeit dominated by the Anglo-Saxon. This assumption, given the context of almost unlimited economic, social, and political opportunity, took much of the sting out of the estrangement that most immigrants felt, going as far back as Michel de Crèvecoeur:

> What attachment can a poor European emigrant have for a country where he had nothing? The knowledge of the language, the love of a few kindred as poor as himself, were the only cords that tied him. His country is now that which gives him land, bread, protection, and consequence. . . . He is either European, or the descendent of a European; hence that strange mixture of blood, which you will find in no other country. . . . He is an American, who, leaving behind him all his ancient prejudices and manners, receives new ones from the new mode of life he has embraced, the new government he obeys and the new rank he holds. . . . Here individuals of all nations are melted into a new race of men, whose labors and posterity will one day cause great

changes in the world. Americans are the western pilgrims, who are
carrying along with them that great mass of arts, sciences, vigor,
and industry, which began long since in the east. They will finish
the great circle.[32]

Until the latter part of the nineteenth century, this easy
absorption of foreign elements through the voluntary abandon-
ment by these groups of their cultural ties was the rule rather
than the exception. The one early exception to the smoothness
of this process was the Catholic minority. As the Common
School movement after 1830 began to pick up impetus, it was
seen as a natural facilitator of the Americanization process. The
Irish and German Catholics coming into America after 1840
were immediately subject to the English linguistic and Protestant religious orthodoxy now perpetuated by the public
schools. The historical result of this early clash over the issue of
religious pluralism was the setting up of the Catholic parochial
school system, with its eventual vindication in the famous
Oregon decision of 1925.

Immigration after 1870 was quite different. Not only was it
larger in absolute number, at times reaching the proportions of
a tidal wave, but the radical change in national origins of the
newer immigrants substantially altered the previous cultural patterns. In spite of the linguistic and religious problems that confronted Irish and German Catholics, these groups did share a
connection with the Anglo-Saxon heritage of the majority of
the population. The newcomers, arriving from Southern or Eastern Europe, crowded into the ghettos of the cities and confronted the prior American tradition with the fact of cultural
heterogeneity on a grand scale. They came not only for the
economic hope offered by America but for the various freedoms America symbolized—religious, social, and political.[33]
They were drawn by the symbol of the Statue of Liberty and its
inscription by Emma Lazarus, "Give me your tired, your poor,
your huddled masses yearning to breathe free."

The fast pace of social and economic change that had

[32] Michel Guillaume St. Jean de Crèvecoeur, "Letters from an American Farmer," (London, 1782), in Oscar Handlin, *Immigration as a Factor
in American History* (Englewood Cliffs, N.J.: Prentice-Hall, Inc., 1959).
[33] R. Freeman Butts and Lawrence A. Cremin, *A History of Education in American Culture* (New York: Holt, Rinehart & Winston, Inc.,
1953), pp. 306-308.

brought European society to the brink of disaster and had precipitated this vast emigration was an international phenomenon.
American society, too, had been changing, under its own impetus. This constant acceleration of change in the American
landscape confused the heretofore calm panorama of American
life. Americans were forced to take a new view of their socioeconomic structure and their role in international political life;
they had to deal with new intellectual currents similar to those
confronted by Dewey.

These currents necessitated, in addition, a serious consideration of the impact of the new immigrants on the American
idea. One of the results was that the same Darwinian intellectual
revolution that had spawned the reformist spirit of such pro-
gressivists as Upton Sinclair, Charles Beard, Thorstein Veblen,
and Oliver Wendell Holmes bred a spirit of reaction, and even
hate, epitomized in certain Social Darwinists and extreme
racists and nationalists.[34]

Anglo-Saxon Nationalism

The challenge to broaden the conception of American
democracy to meet the new contexts of experience was met by
a bitter reaction that focused itself especially upon the values
and culture of the immigrants. This opposition took a number
of forms, varying from outright racism to a mild kind of assimi-
lationism. Perhaps the most blatant of the former was Madison
Grant's exposition in *The Passing of the Great Race*.[35] In this
volume, Grant bemoaned the fact that Nordic man, the American of the earlier era, who represented the highest creation of
Homo sapiens, had, in the tide of humanity now entering the
United States, been degraded by the most primitive elements in
human society, as represented by the other ethnic backgrounds.

This attitude, that the higher values of the Anglo-Saxons
were being dissipated by the culture of the Jews, Latins, and
Slavs, was rather common. It was stated as a scholarly fact by
the noted educational historian Elwood Cubberly, who sadly

[34] See the writings on social Darwinism by Richard Hofstadter, *Social
Darwinism in American Thought* (Philadelphia: University of Pennsylvania
Press, 1944) and Stow Persons, *Evolutionary Thought in America* (New
York: George Braziller, Inc., 1956).

[35] Madison Grant, *The Passing of the Great Race* (New York: Charles
Scribner's Sons, 1916).

cited the racial indigestion that had afflicted America because of the debasing influence of the values of the newcomers:

> These Southern and Eastern Europeans were of a very different type from the North and West Europeans who preceded them. Largely illiterate, docile, often lacking in initiative, and almost wholly without the Anglo-Saxon conceptions of righteousness, liberty, law, order, public decency, and government, their coming has served to dilute tremendously our national stock and to weaken and corrupt our political life. Settling largely in the cities of the North, the agricultural regions of the Middle and the Far West, and the mining districts of the mountain regions, they have created serious problems in housing and living, moral and sanitary conditions, and honest and decent government, while popular education has everywhere been made more difficult by their presence. The result has been that in many sections of our country foreign manners, customs, observances, and language have tended to supplant native ways and the English speech, while the so-called "melting-pot" has had more than it could handle. The new peoples, and especially those from the South and East of Europe, have come so fast that we have been unable to absorb and assimilate them, and our national life, for the past quarter of a century, has been afflicted with a serious case of racial indigestion.[36]

Many demanded a stop to unrestricted immigration, but the needs of our industrial machine for manpower pushed aside these cultural concerns for the time being. In the end, the need to preserve the hegemony of traditional American culture and democracy won out. And the eloquent writings of such as Henry Pratt Fairchild, a New York University sociologist, finally made themselves felt. Typical of this line of argument was the following statement:

> The highest service of America to mankind is to point the way to demonstrate the possibilities, to lead onward to the goal of human happiness. Any force that tends to impair our capacity for leadership is a menace to mankind and a flagrant violation of the spirit of liberalism.
> Unrestricted immigration was such a force. It was slowly, insidiously, irresistibly, eating away the very heart of the United States. What was being melted in the great Melting Pot, losing all form and symmetry, all beauty and character, all nobility and usefulness, was the American nationality itself.[37]

[36] Elwood Cubberly, *Public Education in the United States* (Boston: Houghton Mifflin Company, 1947), pp. 485-486 (written in 1919).

[37] Henry Pratt Fairchild, *The Melting Pot Mistake* (Boston: Little, Brown and Company, 1926), pp. 260-261.

Assimilation

A more moderate view of the challenge of the new minorities presented was the philosophy of the melting pot. Indeed, the largest number of spokesmen for the immigrant groups took up the cry of the melting pot. Israel Zangwill's paean to America probably represented the most optimistic and altruistic feelings of the immigrant as he entered this land with its vaunted heritage of freedom:

> It is the fires of God round His Crucible. There she lies, the great Melting-Pot—listen! Can't you hear the roaring and the bubbling? There gapes her mouth—her harbour where a thousand mammoth feeders come from the ends of the world to pour in their human freight. Ah, what a stirring and a seething! Celt and Latin, Slav and Teuton, Greek and Syrian,—black and yellow,—Jew and Gentile—
>
> Yet, East and West, and North and South, the palm and the pine, the pole and the equator, the crescent and the cross—how the great Alchemist melts and fuses them with his purging flame! Here shall they all unite to build the Republic of Man and the Kingdom of God. Ah, Vera, what is the glory of Rome and Jerusalem where all nations come to worship and look back, compared with the glory of America, where all races and nations come to labour and look forward!
>
> Peace, peace, to all ye unborn millions, fated to fill this great continent—the God of our children give you peace.[38]

From this more tolerant and liberal, albeit theatrical, view of American democracy, the new immigration represented but one more challenge in the creation of a viable nation, not the dread calamity of the dilution of our cultural and racial blood that the racist made out of it.

> A nation is great, not on account of the number of individuals contained within its boundaries, but through the strength begotten of common ideals and aspirations. No nation can exist and be powerful that is not homogeneous in this sense. And the great ethnic problem we have before us is to fuse these diverse elements into one common nationality, having one language, one political practice, one patriotism and one ideal of social development.[39]

[38] Israel Zangwill, *The Melting Pot* (New York, 1909), as quoted in Oscar Handlin, *Immigration as a Factor in American History* (Englewood Cliffs, N.J.: Prentice-Hall, Inc., 1959), p. 150.

[39] Richmond Mayo-Smith, *Emigration and Immigration* (New York, 1904), pp. 77-78, in Oscar Handlin, *Immigration as a Factor in American History* (Englewood Cliffs, N.J.: Prentice-Hall, Inc., 1959), p. 163.

In the vision of the melting pot, the America of tomorrow would be different from that of today: stronger, more malleable, infused with new life and character, because of this new addition of cultures. From it would come one nation, not many, a unified vision of American democracy not fragmented into nationalities, not purely Anglo-Saxon, but the greatest amalgam of that which was best in all the people of the world. The immigrants gave themselves readily to the existing institutions, hopeful of a reciprocity that was existent more in their aspirations than in reality.

Speaking about this problem of assimilation, the Superintendent of Schools of New York City, in 1918, described the educational goals of the schools relative to the values of the immigrants: ". . . broadly speaking, an appreciation of the institutions of this country, absolute forgetfulness of all obligations or connections with other countries because of descent or birth.[40]

Others were more willing to accept the alterations that were to come as a result of the melting pot philosophy. In 1892, James Bryce spoke of the racial qualities of the immigrants changing the character of American society and not necessarily for the bad.[41] Percy Stickney Grant phrased it thus.

> Let us be careful not to put America into the class of the oppressors. Let us rise to an eminence higher than that occupied by Washington or Lincoln, to a new Americanism which is not afraid of the blending in the Western world of races seeking freedom. Our present problem is the greatest in our history. Not colonial independence, not federal unity, but racial amalgamation is the heroic problem of the present, with all it implies in purification and revision of old social, religious, and political ideals, with all its demands in a new sympathy outside of blood and race, and in a willingness to forego old-time privileges.[42]

The assimilationist philosophy was an answer to those who saw the new ethnic stocks as destroyers of traditional Anglo-Saxon values. It was fortunate that, because of their backgrounds and education, many of the immigrants were able to

---

[40] In Horace Kallen, *Culture and Democracy in the United States* (New York: Boni & Liveright, 1924), p. 138.

[41] *Ibid.*, pp. 172–176.

[42] Percy Stickney Grant, "American Ideals and Race Mixture," in *North American Review*, 195 (1912), 513-535, in Oscar Handlin, *op. cit.*

counter the arguments by asserting a different vision of American democracy. But insofar as both of these positions encompassed a vision of the democratic life within the context of a world growing closer together as well as massively industralized and complicated, the simpler vision shone through. Through it, the American society in its newly assimilated form could transcend the rifts and schisms that drove the culturally diverse Europeans into their perennially fratricidal wars. It envisioned a unity in America in which, by giving up his special ethnic, cultural, and national distinctiveness, man could be unified in his cultural purview and thus build political, economic, and social institutions not torn by the enervating contentions of special interests.

Pluralism

As the intellectual persuasiveness of the arguments against the melting pot waned and as emotions of utter prejudice and defensive apology dissipated, men increasingly came to grips with the arguments as to what the American democratic vision was to be. The heavy population increase contributed by East and South Europe made any hope for a purely Anglo-Saxon society chimerical. On the other hand, there was the possibility that the melting-pot theory was in itself an undemocratic position.

Thus the theory that democracy might be equated with a more pluralistic vision of the American ideal began to gain strength among a number of writers, and a more critical examination of the assimilationist views of the melting pot theorists began.

> There is no such thing as humanity in general, into which the definite, heterogeneous, living creature can be melted down. . . . There is no human mould in America to which the spiritual stuff of the immigrant is to be patterned. Not only is there as yet no fixed and final type, but there never can be. . . . The very genius of democracy, moreover, must lead us to desire the widest possible range of variability, the greatest attainable differentiation of individuality, among our population. . . . The business of America is to get rid of mechanical uniformity, and, by encouraging the utmost possible differentiation through mental and psychic cross-fertilization to attain a higher level of humanity.[43]

[43] Horace J. Bridges, "On Becoming an American," in Oscar Handlin, *op. cit.*, pp. 155-158.

Among the leadership of the various ethnic minorities, many began to call out for a greater sense of equality in the treatment of all the contending national values. It was soon understood that the institutions of our society, especially our Anglo-Saxon-oriented schools, could and would undermine the family and neighborhood cultures. The estrangement of youths from their elders, a by-product of the Americanization process, was in itself a poignant aspect of this problem. There arose a quiet demand for at least a greater equality of cultural values within our institutions. The Reverend Enrico Sartorius, speaking about the distaste with which American teachers approached the issue of teaching Italian children about the language and history of Italy, stated:

> By making these children realize that they are connected by blood with a race of glorious traditions, and by adoption have come to belong to a country which has also a glorious past, their love for America will be kept in their hearts without their acquiring a feeling of contempt for their father's country.[44]

Horace Kallen and I. B. Berkson

The most eloquent statements of the pluralist position came from Horace Kallen and I. B. Berkson. Taking much of their philosophical inspiration from the progressive intellectual temper of their times, they attempted to bring the spirit and even the letter of Dewey's philosophy to bear on this issue in which they were each personally involved. Their analysis focused on that crucial element in Dewey's philosophy that equated the democratic society with the opportunities it provided for the fulfillment of individual capacities: "the perfection and conservation of differences." They both noted the manner in which the subtle element of coercion had entered into the melting-pot philosophies, especially as the melting pot had resulted not only in the assimilation of the cultures of the newcomers but also in their digestion and submersion among the institutions of the majority.

Kallen especially derided the patriotic pretensions of such assimilationists as Jacob Riis, Edward Steiner, and Mary Antin, who he said were "intermarried, assimilated even in religion and

---

[44] Reverend Enrico Sartorius, *Social and Religious Life of Italians In America*, in Oscar Handlin, *op. cit.*, pp. 155-158.

more excessively self-consciously flatteringly American than the Americans."[45] The issue seemed to center on the fact that the coercion that was subtly and psychologically exerted to conform people to one pattern of Americanism was basically un-American and undemocratic. Both Kallen and Berkson argued that democracy implied the right of these newcomers to retain the ethnic and cultural affiliation of their choice and therefore not to suffer any debilitating consequences from the exercise of this right. Using Randolph Bourne's phrase, this implied a new American vision—of a "transnational America."

It is on this issue of the status and extent of majority coercion that Berkson and Kallen departed from each other. Although both based their positions on Dewey's philosophical delineation of democracy, pluralism, and individualism, and indeed both quoted Dewey's famous speech in 1916 to the National Education Association, in which he stated that all Americans are hyphenated and that the American is international, interracial, and that our nationalism was a form of internationalism, the ultimate results of their pluralism were quite different.[46]

I. B. Berkson, along with his associate Julius Drachsler, stressed the community theory, which departed in several crucial ways from Kallen's unadulterated pluralism.[47, 48] Berkson's community theory sought to perpetuate those enclaves of individuality that tended naturally to occur within the larger society. These communities are voluntary possibilities but not necessary adjuncts of our nation. Berkson accepts them as existing in a *de facto* manner.

It is not important that some will dissolve because of lack of determination to remain together as cohesive communities. Groups that have no distinctive sense of cultural identity have no reason for staying together.[49] Berkson's greatest concern was

[45] Horace Kallen, *Culture and Democracy in the United States* (New New York: Boni & Liveright, 1924), p. 86.

[46] John Dewey, "Nationalizing Education," in Kallen, *op. cit.*, pp. 131-133.

[47] Isaac B. Berkson, *Theories of Americanization* (New York: Bureau of Publications, Teacher's College, Columbia University, 1920).

[48] Julius Drachsler, *Democracy and Assimilation* (New York: Macmillan Company, 1920).

[49] Berkson, *op. cit.*, p. 103.

that the forces existing in the larger society be neutralized with regard to pressures either to dissolve or perpetuate themselves. If, in the absence of pressures, the community chooses to eliminate itself, we have the melting pot, which he accepts here, "accomplishing the fusion without the evils of hasty assimilation."[50]

There is a sense of national obligation in Berkson's presentation that links his views to the assimilationists, for he ties his communities in with the larger society. Preeminent is this larger society and the unity it symbolizes. Thus, of the Jews, the community to whom he speaks, he reiterates the fact that only over and above their participation in American national life are they Jews.[51] Kallen analyzed Drachsler's and Berkson's panacea as "a sort of ethnic and cultural laissez faire."[52]

Berkson felt no deeper sense of obligation for individual or community than the acceptance of the existing community structure of our land. As he put it, there is no preconceived theory of the individual but one formed "as a result of the interaction of his own nature with the richest environment."[53]

Kallen developed the philosophy of cultural pluralism to its ultimate conclusions. Kallen was unconvinced that anything in the value systems the immigrants brought with them was inimical to the democratic structure of our society. On the contrary, he felt that by adhering strictly to those canons laid down by Dewey, a pluralistic society was the natural result. As Dewey once stated, "Unless local community life can be restored the public cannot adequately resolve its most urgent problem to find and identify itself. But if it be reestablished it will manifest a fullness, variety and freedom of possession and enjoyment of meanings and goods unknown in the contiguous associations of the past."[54] Kallen went even deeper than Dewey in attempting to seek the sources for pluralism. He sought for more than merely a reaction against the deadening monotony of our indus-

[50]*Ibid.*, p. 118.
[51]*Ibid.*, p. 102.
[52]Horace Kallen, *Culture and Democracy in the United States* (New York: Boni & Liveright, 1924), p. 159.
[53]Isaac B. Berkson, *op. cit.*, p. 118.
[54]John Dewey, *The Public and Its Problems* (New York: Henry Holt and Co., 1927), p. 216.

trialized society and saw that national diversification had to be extended from the individual to the group.[55]

Kallen, to be sure, felt with Dewey that democracy was linked with the concept of semi-independent and autonomous publics interacting on the important issues of experience. Kallen, however, believed that to be meaningful the publics had to be richer in organization than the superficial political, economic, and geographic ties that brought men into communities. He saw this deeper interaction in the ethnic minorities of his time. Much later in life he approvingly quoted Florian Znaniecki's statement that "a solidary human collectivity of hundreds of thousands, even millions of people who share the same culture can exist for a long time without a common political government."[56]

Kallen argued that the basic principle of human and indeed of biological existence is diversity.[57] This diversity is absorbed by the child through the family in the first years of his life. Allowed to express their inner freedom, humans will separate into culturally distinct groups. It is only the technological and economic setting of society that superimposes homogeneity. If one only examines man's so-called useless activities, the true heterogeneity of human existence becomes apparent. In his late work, *Cultural Pluralism and the American Idea,* Kallen used this concept to divide man's existence into a daytime period, when he works in an environment of sameness, and an evening period, in which a rich diversity is the rule.[58]

Throughout his early writings, Kallen's theme revolved around assimilation and the coercive powers of society. Just as all prior oppressions have been overcome, so will the uniformalizing effect of our institutions.

> What is important, however, is the fact that the uniformity is superimposed, not inwardly generated. Under its regimentation the diversities persist; upon it and by means of it they grow. But instead of growing freely, and fusing by their own expansion into

---

[55] Kallen, *op. cit.,* p. 130. Kallen uses several insights of Norman Hapgood for this thought.

[56] Horace Kallen, *Cultural Pluralism and the American Idea* (Philadelphia: University of Pennsylvania Press, 1956), p. 45.

[57] Kallen, *Culture and Democracy in the United States* (New York: Boni & Liveright, 1924), p. 120.

[58] *Ibid.,* passim.

contact and harmony with their peers, they grow distortedly, as
reactions against and compensations for the superimposed unity.
In the end they must win free, for Nature is naturally pluralistic;
her unities are eventual, not primary; mutual adjustments not
regimentations of superior force. Human institutions have the
same character. Where there is no mutuality there may be "law
and order" but there cannot be peace.[59]

Kallen proposed a union of nationalities on the model of
Great Britain and Switzerland. In keeping with Dewey's viewpoint, natural rights as they are conceived in Switzerland seem
to operate as generalizations from the data of human nature.
Men may change wines or clothes, but they cannot change their
grandfathers.[60] The concept of race enters very strongly into
his position. He was, however, vague on the exact connotations
of the term "race." It is probable that he used it broadly to
denote deep cultural and historical ties rather than specific biological or genetic structures.

He was convinced that the pluralistic needs of man are
rooted so deeply in his nature that they cannot be eliminated.
They can only go underground. Thus, by their indifference, the
laissez-faire community theory and the melting-pot position
violate certain basic demands of man. Kallen followed Dewey's
views of a hyphenated America, a transnational nation, and
added the opinion that the more racial strains there are, the
greater the American nationality, "they are more national to
the degree that they attain to the perfect utterance of their race
and place."[61]

Kallen's dream was of an America consisting of a number of
nationalities federated to the larger nation much as the states
were united into one nation. There would not be the need for
regional or political, but for cultural differentiation. Kallen
sensed man's deep desires to retain his special ethnic culture. He
realized that the various theories of Americanization were
merely variants of a new antidemocratic assault on the sanctity
of the individual. Dewey's dictum that the needs of individual
fulfillment were a sacrosanct aspect of the true democracy was
thus fully applied by Kallen to the contextual circumstances
surrounding the incoming flood of immigrants.

[59] Kallen, *op. cit.*, pp. 178-179.
[60] *Ibid.*, pp. 121-123.
[61] *Ibid.*, pp. 211-226.

DEWEY AND THE FAILURE OF CULTURAL PLURALISM

The Decline of Cultural Pluralism

There were few to share this special vision. It was as if a theoretical blindness to the fact and value of culture allowed men to ignore its importance to the individual. Just as men were at one time blind to the facts of social class or economics as determiners of the freedom of some and the degradation of others, the intellectuals turned away from cultural values and therefore from pluralism. Their interest was focused on the externals of men, on what people wore and in what material circumstances they lived and worked. At that time, the need seemed to lie in breaking down the special economic and social privileges that separated people rather than in succoring their cultural differences.

Thus the philosophy of cultural pluralism gradually disappeared as the tremendous pressures of society for assimilation were brought to bear on the immigrants. Economic, educational, and social opportunities were presented to all men from those national institutions where the American orthodoxy was centered. The Great Depression and the New Deal that followed, focused as they were on the matter of economic survival, further weakened the intensity of ethnic feeling. World War II, in which differences were patriotically anathema, certainly brought Kallen's expectation that the drive for pluralism would go underground to a disillusioning conclusion. People did not take their struggle for pluralism underground. What eventually occurred was that the homogeneous mass society, which Kallen and Dewey saw as the danger to man, produced its own form of underground, a psychosocial underground characterized by neuroses, crime, delinquency, and alienation.

Cultural pluralism as an explicit value has not rooted itself in our society. In part, the explanation can be found in the changing social and technological conditions of our century. However, if we believe that ideas have an impact on human actions, then we must also place some of the responsibility on defects in the philosophy of pragmatism.

Though he was a supporter of pluralism, Dewey failed to contribute the intellectual elements that could have helped win it a place in our nation. Dewey did put forth the view that a democracy needs a plurality of publics to nourish a truer individualism. He realized that democracy connotes a society that transcends the formal, legal constraints against the abuse of individual rights; democracy implies a society that approaches its problems through scientific canons of rationality. In this way the whole enterprise of social living is given potential clarity and specificity. It is a philosophical vision with marvelous potential for creating real choices in the random, rather chaotic processes of traditional democratic action.

It is at this point that the difficulties in Dewey's position become evident. Dewey urged us to use scientific forms of rationality to confront our contemporary problems and to solve them in a manner that would increase individual choice and realize the potentialities in each person. But as a matter of fact, when we do confront issues, we are always involved in a confusing nexus of choices. The evidence is rarely clear as to which of the possible decisions could lead us towards our goals of individual realization.[62]

Here we are faced with a correlative difficulty. What are our goals? If we know them we may choose more wisely as we proceed towards them. Dewey said that the small community is an important value. He favored publics in which men are never means for external economic and industrial ends but are educated so that they can determine the intelligent use of these institutions. It is our contention that to predicate our day-to-day pragmatic decisions on the basis of a vague belief in the validity of publics, of small enclaves of pluralism, is not enough. We need to know why we should do so, and what the character of these pluralities is to be. A richer substantive envisagement of the plural society is needed. Dewey did not give us this vision. As J. H. Robinson stated, "Dewey and the Progressives had no reforms to propose except the liberation of intelligence."[63]

Dewey implied that the plural society does not exist as an end in itself. Rather it is the best social arrangement for leading us on to more changes *ad infinitum.* Change, according to Dewey, is basic to the structure of the universe. This assump-

---

[62] Morton White, *Social Thought in America* (Boston: Beacon Press, 1957), pp. 243-246.
[63] Quoted in Morton White, *Social Thought in America* (Boston: Beacon Press, 1957), p. 194.

tion provides the metaphysical justification for his views on social change. The community concept in itself contains Dewey's ideal of growth for the sake of growth, which was made into one of the more important leitmotifs of progressive education. The community, or public, as Dewey envisioned it, is an instrument through which scientific reasoning may be advanced, especially in making the economic, political, and social decisions that were so central a part of Dewey's view of experience.

To postulate goals that we might use as a sightline for day-to-day pragmatic decisions might be a valid methodological procedure on the basis of Dewey's philosophy. But Dewey himself was unwilling to make a specific commitment to any tangible democratic goals.[64] The closest he came to a direct involvement in current issues was his general critique of our contemporary economic institutions. The object of these criticisms was the spurious and outdated individualism of modern capitalism and the robber-baron psychology it precipitated.

Dewey's commitment to a more socialized view of economics was implied in the antithesis he set up between biological individualism and the demands of sociality. In real life, it meant that the anarchic individualism of the nineteenth century had degenerated into a conspiratorial society whose inevitable outcome, the Great Depression, was evidence of the need for a more rational organization of man's economic affairs.

But this is an incomplete resolution to the problem of how far, how long, and to what extent we should socialize. And how does this fit into the pluralized society, of which Dewey was also a staunch proponent? That there were few answers to these questions was in part due to the fact that Dewey's scientific understanding of human nature and the manner in which society was related to man's nature were not fully delineated. The entire superstructure of Dewey's method of science and his views on democracy, which contain dramatically perceptive solutions, still rested on an incomplete metaphysical basis.[65]

The little that Dewey spoke about the values that bring people together or should bring them together are couched in a

[64] White, *op. cit.,* pp. 243-246.
[65] See W. T. Jones' criticisms of Dewey in *History of Western Philosophy* (New York: Harcourt, Brace & World, 1952), pp. 953-965.

vague terminology that refers to the deeper social relations from which, for example, religiosity emanates.[66] His proposals for the democratic society are negative in that they are only therapeutic and methodological. The therapy consists of ridding men of their inherited and encrusted dogmatic beliefs and institutions. The methodology derives from Dewey's belief that once an individual accepts the logic of science, any confrontation between individual and experience will ultimately result in good works. The human being now has a decision making method that is the correlative of lower organic forms of instinctual survival.

Dewey maintained that men do not come together because they share any special human capacity in itself good, but because of a practical need to find a means of achieving the elusive temporary ends of life. As long as the universe lays novelty before him man will need to adapt to this novelty. Science is the means for this adaptation, for it utilizes the heretofore latent possibilities of human intelligence.

It is no wonder that Dewey's philosophy has always evidenced an underlying ambivalence to the opposing ideas of unification and pluralism. And it is no accident that the so-called cult of social adjustment in its most extravagant misinterpretations resulted in such blatantly conformist tendencies in the schools. It is this ambivalence that failed Kallen and Berkson, each of whom in a sense based his own perspective on pluralism on the instrumentalism of Dewey.

In reality, there are no roots in Dewey's philosophy for a consideration of the real significance of differences in cultural outlooks.[67] He is so interested in human thought and actions as instrumental to adaptive behavior that he has virtually omitted from his vision the significance of the uniquenesses of culture. Even his study of art never went deeply into esthetic experience; it merely touched on the surface of art. He took for granted its existence as a social phenomenon and showed how it could be incorporated into the rhythm of social life for all men rather than be used as an embellishment for a leisured class.[68]

    [66] John Dewey, *A Common Faith* (New Haven: Yale University Press, 1934).
    [67] Isaac B. Berkson, *The Ideal and the Community* (New York: Harper & Row, Publishers, 1958), pp. 48-49.
    [68] John Dewey, *Art as Experience* (New York: Minton Balch, 1935), pp. 344-349.

Art was truly an important aspect of life to him, but Dewey did not elaborate on its structure and function. He acknowledged the tremendous differences in the artistic qualities of the various cultures, but he did not attempt to explain the differences. In addition, Dewey often speaks of consummatory experiences such as art, self-satisfying in themselves. Yet in the context of his general philosophy, the consummatory experience seems rootless and unaccounted for.

Most crucial, Dewey did not come to grips with the fact that scientific logic, which he felt was the great hope for the democratic life, strives for unity, for public truths, whereas cultures produce unique truths or values. This difficulty is heightened when we recall that Dewey polemicized constantly against the divisive sectarianism of religion as opposed to the social unification of science.[69] That this view of knowledge and society is clearly antithetical to a commitment to pluralism except in a narrow structural sense, i.e., political, is evidenced in Berkson's acute criticisms of Dewey. The emphasis Berkson placed on the stable discipline of traditional community values as a guard against the egoistic, individualistic tendencies in Dewey reflects his continuing concern with the implicit difficulties of the pluralistic aspects of Dewey's instrumentalism.[70]

A Contemporary Challenge

The philosophy of pluralism is now presented with opportunities of a new sort. While the old ethnic groups are in the main vitiated in their self-consciousness and social structure, they still exist amidst other equally venerable, yet active, pluralities within our social structure.[71] In addition, new minorities have made themselves felt. The Negro, Puerto Rican, and Mexican have been placed in the traditional position of the undigested minorities—now made more difficult because of racial complications.

Great opportunity inheres in this new sociocultural challenge. The challenge has outdistanced the economic and politi-

---

[69] Dewey, *A Common Faith* (New Haven: Yale University Press, 1934), p. 26.

[70] Isaac B. Berkson, *op. cit.*, pp. 48-51, 60-61.

[71] Ethel M. Albert, "Conflict and Change in American Values: A Cultural-Historical Approach," *Ethics* (October 1963), pp. 13-33. On page 26, Dr. Albert remarks on the tenacity of older cultural minorities as well as the fecundity of our society in producing new sects.

cal fears of the pragmatists even though the recent population expansion fitted into the absorptive economic demands of the new institutional structure of the mass society. Dewey was basically correct in his fears for the structure of our democratic polity. The challenge to democracy, however, is now psychosocial, resulting from the type of irrationality generated by institutions over which individuals have no control.

The danger today is not the typical economic, political, or social authoritarianism of the past, but the subtle authoritarianism bred into our social system by these mass institutions: communicative, political, economic, philanthropic, and educational. The fearful results of the breakdown in the mass society, as earlier noted, can be seen in the example of Nazi Germany, certainly the unparalleled example of a psychosocial political sickness in the history of mankind. The important implication of the mass society, which Dewey would have no doubt perceived, is that, as now structured, it cannot support the democracy of our aspirations. Dwight MacDonald has contrasted this inherent defect of mass society and culture with a community in which values and ideals can be shared and human needs and concerns succored and developed:

> There are theoretical reasons why Mass Culture is not and can never be any good. I take it as axiomatic that culture can only be produced by and for human beings. But in so far as people are organized (more strictly disorganized) as masses, they lose their human identity and quality. For the masses are in historical time what a crowd is in space: a large quantity of people unable to express themselves as human beings because they are related to one another neither as individuals nor as members of communities—indeed, they are not related *to each other* at all, but "to something distant, abstract, non-human: a football game or bargain sale in the case of a crowd, a system of industrial production, a party or a state in the case of the masses." The mass man is a solitary atom, uniform with and undifferentiated from thousands and millions of other atoms who go to make "the lonely crowd" as David Riesman well calls American society. A folk or a people, however, is a community, i.e., a group of individuals linked to each other by common interests, work, traditions, values, and sentiments; something like a family, each of whose members has a special place and function as an individual while at the same time sharing the group's interests (family budget) sentiments (family quarrels) and culture (family jokes). The scale is small enough so that it "makes a difference" what the

individual does, a first condition for human—as against mass existence. He is at once more important as an individual than in a
mass society and at the same time more closely integrated into
the community, his creativity nourished by a rich combination of
individualism and communalism (the great culture-bearing elites
of the past have been communities of this kind). In contrast a
mass society, like a crowd, is so undifferentiated and loosely
structured that its atoms, in so far as human values go, tend to
cohere only along the line of the least common denominator; its
morality sinks to that of its most brutal and primitive members,
its taste to that of the least sensitive and most ignorant. And in
addition to everything else, the scale is simply too big, there are
just *too many people.*[72]

Dewey has taken us along the path toward a recognition of the value of a pluralistic conception of society for a
democratic philosophy of man. He has also shown us the intimate relevance of the educational system of a society as a prime
tool for the creation of democracy. In a sense the school is the
microcosm of the larger social endeavor. If the ideas promulgated for pluralism can work in the school, which is a relatively
controlled environment—a social laboratory—then it may also
work in society. But before we can consider pluralism as an
educational philosophy we must establish the philosophical
issues that need further exploration and amplification. We need
to confront explicitly those weaknesses in Dewey's philosophy
with alternate and supplementing concepts.

There are a number of problems that have to be restated
and reinterpreted within a new philosophic frame if pluralism is
to be revived, and to stand on grounds that are intellectually
acceptable to intelligent men. The attention that Dewey focused on the practical, problem-solving aspects of man needs to
be altered in its primary status as a defining aspect of human
nature. Dewey was permanently converted by the persuasiveness of Darwin's teachings. Although he was not a strict behav-
iorist, his views of society and science were colored by these
biological commitments. We now need to have more and better
reasons for splitting up into pluralities than to provide for a
more efficient means of handling man's practical adaptation

[72] Dwight MacDonald, "A Theory of Mass Culture," *Diogenes* (Sum-
mer 1953), pp. 1-17. Reprinted with permission of the Macmillan Company from Bernard Rosenberg and David M. White (eds.), *Mass Culture.*
Copyright © by The Free Press, a Corporation, 1957, pp. 69-70.

problems through the use of scientific method. Ultimately we must search for the deeper sources of pluralism in culture and then to fix the status of science within a broader social perspective.

Even the concept of individualism must be amplified beyond Dewey's views. If democracy exists for the realization of the latent potentialities of each person, then these potentialities must have a more substantial significance than individual thinking for increased problem-solving abilities. The depth of meaning of cultural identity has yet to be satisfactorily plumbed. Indeed, what we cherish about the individuality of cultures themselves are the nonpractical aspects—the arts, cuisine, literature, style, and architecture.[73]

Human nature might be better understood were it examined from the standpoint of its manifold social characteristics. Pluralism is as basic to human nature and needs as is freedom of thought and expression. Pluralism, to be sure, is only a mechanism in society, a social superstructure representing a hypothesis about the manner in which men ought to be able to organize and pattern their social institutions. Its democratic implications derive from the expectations that a structural mode of social living can have some effect on the natural cultural expressions of men, and that these expressions are relevant, if not indeed crucial, to the attainment by each individual of his natural human rights. No philosophy can legislate truth, democracy, or happiness for men. What it can do is to provide intellectual guidelines for social action, which, when effected in society, will stimulate men to use their given capacities to achieve what is most dear to their existence.

True, there were limitations to Dewey's philosophy, as there will be to any set of ideas placed in a context of history. To his lasting credit, however, Dewey left to us a precise understanding of the instrumentalist role of any philosophical analysis.

[73] Horace Kallen, *Culture and Democracy in the United States* (New York: Boni & Liveright, 1924), p. 181; *Cultural Pluralism and the American Idea* (Philadelphia: University of Pennsylvania Press, 1956), passim.

chapter 3

Ernst Cassirer
and the Sources
of Cultural Thought

THE PROBLEM OF KNOWLEDGE

Darwin and Pragmatism

As has been noted innumerable times, the philosophy of pragmatism was a peculiarly American phenomenon. From its origins with C. S. Peirce, William James, and John Dewey, pragmatism has represented an era in American intellectual thought that was conditioned by one of the great archetypal ideas of modern time, the theory of biological evolution as developed by Charles Darwin and his successors. Evolutionary theory spanned a series of cognate theories in disciplines as disparate as economics, sociology, psychology, and education. Indeed, the progressive movement in education developing at the end of the nineteenth century in a context of industrial expansion adopted a mild version of the evolving scientism of that period. Through the aegis of Edward Thorndike and William Heard Kilpatrick, it became committed to a behavioral and social adaptational approach.

This commitment was part of a general national intellectual purview. It was difficult to see, with our efficient exploitation of natural resources for technological control of the environment, any other meaning to human existence than that given in the adaptational and materialistic perspective.

But as could have been expected, conditions of life have changed in the interval. Such new and exciting ideas as pragmatism eventually age, seem redundant and passé. The discontinuities inherent in any set of ideas have become more glaring and in need of confrontation. Progressive education, social Darwinism, even B. F. Skinner's behavioristic psychology were or are in the process of being consigned to their historic interments.

Man requires new sets of ideas to help illuminate his conditions. Yet we can expect that these too will eventually follow the old into the textbooks of philosophy and the history of ideas. With the demise of the pragmatic tradition in the United States, the weakening of Marxism in Europe, and the quickening pace of social change throughout the world, it is understandable that we are now in search of a secure philosophy to enlighten us as to our movement and direction. We have created a pattern of determining social policy by reacting to each succeeding precipitating event. This has resulted in an almost rudderless set of social programs. We can thus appreciate the increased interest in heretofore ignored European philosophical trends such as phenomenology and existentialism.

To a certain degree the suspicions of the efficacy of the Deweyan tradition for long-range postulations as well as for deeper assessments of human nature and society are responsible for the American attitude toward philosophy and planning. From the standpoint of planning for a more pluralistic and heterogeneous culture, these attitudes have been fatal.

The impact of Darwinism was almost totally westward, continental Europe being relatively untouched. Thus, whereas for Dewey, from 1890 on, Darwinism was an *a priori* commitment of his thought, the theory of evolution became significant for the structure of Ernst Cassirer's philosophy only at the end of his career, after he had arrived in America. Cassirer's perspective on knowledge, man, and society had quite different intellectual sources in spite of the fact that both Dewey and he arrived at rather similar views on a number of substantive philosophical issues. Cassirer was one of the few European philosophers respected by Dewey and whom he did not lump with the traditional class of "German metaphysicians."

The usefulness of Cassirer's philosophy as a supplement to the pluralistic tradition in America does not lie in any explicit pluralistic position. He did not officially refer to such issues. Yet his views, and those of his important American disciple

Susanne Langer, on knowledge, culture, and human thought constitute the most important intellectual support for a pluralistic social and cultural position that has as yet been promulgated.

An important methodological consideration to be emphasized is that in his knowledge and appreciation of the sciences, Cassirer has no peer. He was perhaps better versed even than Dewey in his firsthand knowledge of a number of empirical disciplines. Finally, he was continuously sensitive to the contextual significance of science, allowing the evidence to determine the evolution of his theoretical vision.

The Origin of Cassirer's Philosophy

Ernst Cassirer, born in Breslau in 1874, received his philosophical training at the University of Marburg under the tutelage of Hermann Cohen. This university was one of a number of neo-Kantian schools of idealism that flourished in France and Germany at the end of the nineteenth and early in the twentieth century. The Marburg Kantians were engaged in a reappraisal of the philosophy of Immanuel Kant (1724-1804) in the context of the great late-nineteenth-century surge in the physical sciences.[1] According to their view, a reevaluation of Kantianism was necessary because of the renewed interest of scientists in the Koenigsberg philosopher. This interest was especially keen since the decline of Hegel's influence in European philosophy.

The particular preoccupation of the Marburgers was the theory of knowledge. Their concern was to see how current speculations among scientists such as Mach, Helmholtz, and Hertz on the nature of physical theory could be clarified and be incorporated into the philosophical system Kant set forth in his various writings.

This preoccupation with the historical roots of the theory of knowledge, especially the debt owed to Kant, was an important aspect of Cassirer's writings. It was this historical interest that led him to elaborate on the Marburg school's exclusive concern with knowledge in the physical and mathematical

---

[1] Dimitry Gawronsky, "Ernst Cassirer: His Life and His Work," in Paul A. Schilpp (ed.), *The Philosophy of Ernst Cassirer* (New York: Tudor Publishing Co., 1949), pp. 1-37.

realm, to include the problems of culture. But it is essential to understand that the basic insights of Kant, as Cassirer interpreted them, never left him as an intellectual guide.

The Marburg Kantians saw Kant's self-appointed task as that of establishing the philosophical rationale for the commonly accepted belief in the truths of Newtonian physics.[2] Kant's first major work, The *Critique of Pure Reason*, purported to explain the manner and reasons by which we all come to similar scientific conclusions regarding the nature of physical motion.[3] In his philosophical perspective, Kant eschewed both historical philosophical extremes: the rationalists' grasping for a reality in thought beyond the realm of sense experience and the empiricists' reduction of all knowledge to a scattering of sensory moments explained by superficial and gratuitous regulatory constructs. He recognized the need for

> . . . the avoidance of the two extreme positions which would cause us to oscillate between a scepticism which doubts science because of the failure of metaphysics and a dogmatism which finds in the successful application of our *a priori* categories in science a justification for their application in a region where they cannot be applied successfully. The two evils can be permanently removed only by a critical philosophy which shows that the categories can be proved, but only for the kind of objects which we encounter in science and ordinary experience.[4]

Kant's solution—which has been labeled his Copernican revolution in the theory of knowledge—substituted for the traditional search for a reality external to the mind of man, an enquiry concerning the conditions and elements involved in the production of the kind of knowledge gained in Newtonian science. In this view, the apparent characteristics of scientific reality were to be attributed to the manner in which this reality was constructed from the experience of the knower through the active synthetic workings of the human mind. It followed that knowledge was a product not only of those presumed external

2 Ernst Cassirer, *Kant's Leben und Lehre* (Berlin, 1918); also Gottfried Martin, *Kant's Metaphysics and Theory of Science*, trans. P. G. Lucas (Manchester: University of Manchester Press, 1955).
    3 Trans. Norman Kemp-Smith (London, 1958), originally written 1781 (1st ed.), 1787 (2d ed.).
    4 A. C. Ewing, "A Short Commentary on *Kant's Critique of Pure Reason*" (Chicago: University of Chicago Press, 1938), p. 12.

sensations received by the sensory organs but also of the human mind's capacity to give order and meaning to experience.

At this point in the delineation of the Kantian tradition, the Marburg school pointed to the crucial critical lesson in Kant's *Critique of Pure Reason.* It felt that we must eschew all metaphysical attempts to interpret the Kantian philosophy as a search for *"das Ding an sich"* (the thing in itself) as it might exist outside of human knowing. Likewise, we must bypass the problem of psychology, i.e., the question of how the mind organizes sensory materials into concepts. As Adamson, interpreting Kant's program, phrases it, "He is not asking with Locke, whence the details of experience arise, he is attempting a natural history of the growth of experience in the individual mind," and in this is attempting to "state exhaustively what conditions are necessarily involved in any fact of knowledge, i.e., in any synthetic combination of parts of experience by the subject."[5]

Kant thus turned from questions concerning the nature of ultimate reality or the ultimate objects of knowledge to investigate the laws, processes, and forms of knowledge. For Kant, space and time were not to be regarded as things but as sources of knowledge. He did not see them as independent objects that are somehow present and that we can master by experiment and observation. He saw them as conceptual "conditions of the possibility of experience," rather than as things. The critical concerns of Kantianism, as regards the knowledge we derive from experience, lay with form and function, not with substance and reality.[6]

With this philosophical foundation in Kantianism, Cassirer confronted one of the most important philosophical debates of his time, the controversy over the nature and status of physical theory.[7] Many physicists of the time were attempting to understand the role and status of the theories they were so fruitfully exploiting. Some, including Weber and Kelvin, conceived of the Newtonian laws of motion as a reflection of ultimate reality.

[5] Robert Adamson, "Kant," *Encyclopaedia Britannica,* 11th ed., 1910–1911, Vol. 15, p. 668. Reprinted with permission.

[6] Ernst Cassirer, *The Philosophy of Symbolic Forms* (New Haven: Yale University Press, 1953). Vol. 1, p. 79.

[7] First systematically confronted by Cassirer in *Substance and Function* in 1910 (New York: Dover Publications, Inc., 1953).

Others, including Mach, Ostwald, and Helm, rejected the metaphysical claims of the mechanists with extreme empiricist arguments. According to Helm, for example, "There exist neither atoms, nor energy nor any kind of concept, but only those experiences immediately derived from direct observation.[8] The philosophical debate was reminiscent of the quarrels between the continental rationalists and the English empiricists of the previous century. Indeed, the time appeared to be ripe for the entrance of a new Kant to resolve the issue.

What did occur was the gradual rediscovery and utilization of Kant's critical arguments by a number of scientists, from Helmholtz and Zeller to Poincaré and Hertz.[9] It was in this context that the Marburg neo-Kantians, Hermann Cohen, Paul Natorp, and finally Ernst Cassirer, in the last decades of the nineteenth century, added their voices to the discussion. They concerned themselves with a detailed examination of the inner structure of physical theory, and underscored its conventional character. To them, theory did not reflect the external structure of reality, nor could it be reduced to a scattering of sensations or perceptions. Their *leitmotif* was the creative function of the human mind in theory building.

These thinkers rejected all absolutistic interpretations of the constituent principles and axioms of a theory. For these constituents, according to the Marburg school, consisted of a series of judgmental orientations related to the empirical elements that make up the matter of the theory. Thus such factors as space and time in Newtonian science necessitated reinterpretation in Einstein's general theory of gravitation. The supposed *a priori* interpretation of Euclidean geometry, as found in Newton, was rendered obsolete by relativity theory, and a new integration of space and time was constructed.[10] The lesson of relativity theory with regard to the metaphysical claims in

---

[8] G. Helm, quoted in Ernst Cassirer, *The Problem of Knowledge*, trans. W. H. Woglom and C. W. Hendel (New Haven: Yale University Press, 1950), p. 100.

[9] Ernst Cassirer, "Neo-Kantianism," *Encyclopaedia Britannica*, 14th ed., pp. 214-216.

[10] See Ernst Cassirer, *Einstein's Theory of Relativity*, trans. M. Swabey (New York: Tudor Publishing Co., 1953); also I. K. Stephens, "Cassirer's Doctrine of the A Priori," in Paul A. Schilpp (ed.), *The Philosophy of Ernst Cassirer* (New York: Tudor Publishing Co., 1949), pp. 156-158.

mechanics was conclusive. Henceforth, no one would confuse the character of the so-called *a priori* invariants (Euclidean geometry) of the created theory with metaphysical judgments about the nature of reality.[11] The former constitutes a logical problem for epistemology, the latter a speculative judgment having a different, perhaps a poetic, function.

Cassirer and the other members of the Marburg school came to their conclusions concerning the nature of scientific knowledge as a result of their study of the historical development of physical science. Cassirer did not at first present a unique vision of the nature of knowledge, but one that was culled from the work of the theoreticians in science and applied to philosophy. It was the scientists who achieved the critical symbolic vision of scientific knowledge. Hertz, Poincaré, and Duhem came to these conclusions independently.

This interpretation stipulated that any theory of science represents a free creative transformation of the data of experience into the realm of scientific possibility. Scientific knowledge is "the expression of a highly complex intellectual process —a process in which theorizing holds full sway in order to attain to its goal through experience and therein to find confirmation or justification."[12] The laws of science are used as a criterion of experience, not derived directly from experience. As Poincaré put it, "They are not so much assertions about empirical facts as maxims by which we interpret those facts in order to bring them together into a complete and coherent whole."[13]

Thus scientific theory was understood as a symbolic creation of man, to be used as a logical criterion for the evaluation of experience. The role of scientific theory was to be an instrumental one; its function was to unite the various aspects of human experience, natural and contrived (experimental) under the rule of laws. These laws were to be so grouped as to form an ever larger pattern of universal regularities. Man was striving once again to encompass all his experiences under one great theory. Perhaps this was the meaning of Einstein's search

[11] Felix Kaufman, "Cassirer's Theory of Scientific Knowledge," in Paul A. Schilpp, (ed.), *op. cit.*, pp. 191-193.
[12] Ernst Cassirer, *The Problem of Knowledge*, trans. W. H. Woglom and C. W. Hendel (New Haven: Yale University Press, 1950), p. 106.
[13] *Ibid.*

for a unified field theory, one that would bring together under one general law the various domains of physics.

According to the symbolic theory proposed by Cassirer, science did not reveal the nature of reality. It was a creation of the human mind built from the interaction of man's sensory organs with external experience and synthesized by the innate capacities of the human mind. As Kant had proposed in his critical teachings, when we examine knowledge created by the "human mind experiencing," we are involved in a discussion that has logical, not psychological or metaphysical, dimensions. The structure of knowledge is not to be confused with the processes of acquisition and production of knowledge.

Cassirer's investigation into the nature of scientific thought brought him to the same conclusion, and at about the same time, as did John Dewey's inquiry into the nature of scientific intelligence. Both philosophers established to their satisfaction that scientific theory is essentially instrumentalist in nature. It is a tool that man has freely chosen to use; it is not forced upon him by exterior and predetermined conditions. The important difference between the two is that Dewey's conclusion came from an essentially biological and psychological set of insights ultimately derived from Darwin, while Cassirer's views came from an internal logical analysis of the structure of physical theory inspired by the Kantianism of the Marburg philosophers.

Cassirer was now able to refocus his thinking upon man, the creature who created science. If science had some significance for Cassirer beyond its purely instrumental character of leading us to organize experience into wider and more universal relationships formed by the various aspects of sensory experience, it was that man had created it. Cassirer concluded that the quest for an understanding of experience was a primary and deeply ingrained need of man. The historic search that finally resulted in modern science was part of this need. As a product of human culture, science had been prepared for through the millenia in common-sense language and then in philosophical thought. [14] Science was thus but the latest manifestation of a trend evident in human culture since its inception. It was the fulfillment of

[14] Ernst Cassirer, *The Philosophy of Symbolic Forms*, trans. Ralph Manheim (New Haven: Yale University Press, 1953), Vol. III.

what must be a basic capacity and need of man—that of organizing experience into cores of increasingly universal meaning (laws, regularities).

At a crucial period in Cassirer's development, when he had completed not only some of his most renowned historical studies in philosophy but also his earliest systematic work in the philosophy of science, *Substance and Function* (1910), which was the first important statement of his symbolic-functional view of the nature of science, he felt the need for a larger elaboration of this theme.[15] One day in Berlin in 1917, Cassirer suddenly came to realize the significance and the larger dimensions of the problem of knowledge.[16] It was the peculiar psychological tenor of Germany and the midcontinent in those war-filled days that finally turned Cassirer's attention to a reconsideration of the social environment. He had always been sensitive to the significance of the arts, literature, and religious feelings for man's social and cultural life. In looking at his contemporary environment, dominated not by the ethos of scientific enquiry but by the incipient fears and rampant irrationalities of his day, Cassirer was moved to reconsider the status of these cultural phenomena together with their relationship to the scientific activity of man.

Cassirer grappled with the following problem: Must we view man's cultural life as one divided between the rational symbolic constructs of science and the patently irrational behavior demonstrated in politics, religion, and social behavior? May it not be true that, just as man organizes his sensory experiences in formed conceptual meanings in the pursuit of scientific knowledge, the scattered sensations that he continuously encounters can also be ordered into conceptual constructs in the other areas of cultural life? As Carl Hamburg has phrased it, may there not be many forms of thought in which there is sense in the senses (*Sinnerfüllung im Sinnlichen*)?[17]

The question has been succinctly phrased by Susanne

[15] Ernst Cassirer, *Das Erkenntnisproblem in der Philosophie und Wissenschaft der Neuen Zeit* (Berlin: Bruno Cassirer, 1906 (Vol. I) and 1907 (Vol. II).

[16] Dimitry Gawronsky, in Paul A. Schilpp (ed.), *The Philosophy of Ernst Cassirer* (New York: Tudor Publishing Co., 1949), p. 25.

[17] Carl Hamburg, *Symbol and Reality: Studies in the Philosophy of Ernst Cassirer* (The Hague: Martinus Nijhoff, 1956), pp. 59-60.

Langer. Writing in 1943, in a new age of stress and travail, she published *Philosophy in a New Key*, which extended and reinforced the philosophical viewpoint initiated by Cassirer:

> A philosophy that knows only deductive or inductive logic as reason and classes all other human functions as "emotive," "irrational" and "animalian" can see only regression to a prelogical state in the present passionate and unscientific ideologies. All it can show us as the approach to Parnassus is the way of factual data, hypotheses, trial, judgement and generalization. All other things our minds do are dismissed as irrelevant to intellectual progress, they are residues, emotional disturbances, or throwbacks to animal estate.
>
> But a theory of mind whose keynote is the symbolic function, whose problem is the morphology of significance, is not obliged to draw that bifurcating line between science and folly. It can see those ructions and upheavals of the modern mind not as a lapse of rational interest caused by animal impulse but as the exact contrary—as a new phase of savagedom indeed but inspired by the rational need of envisagement and understanding.[18]

In looking back upon his studies in the development of scientific knowledge, Cassirer saw science as but one of many products of man's cultural experience. Common-sense language, myth, religion, and the various art forms are all products of the same basic constituents of experience—the encounter of the human being with the variety of sensory impressions that his brain is equipped to synthesize into meaningful signs.

Thus the function of a philosophy dealing with the cultural facts of our world would be to unravel the particular meaning and structure of these heretofore supposedly chaotic forms. Behind the philosophical extension of Cassirer's position on the epistemological status of scientific theory lay this conviction that meaning and order could be found in all human sensory experience. However, the meanings and structure of art or the religious interpretations of experience are necessarily different from those of scientifically significant symbols.

In effect what Cassirer had uncovered was a covert axiom of common-sense belief, that such areas of culture as art, religion, and language are irreducible to the value and logical systems of

¹⁸Susanne Langer, *Philosophy in a New Key* (Cambridge: Harvard University Press, 1957), pp. 292-293.

discursive knowledge. These areas of culture are intrinsic. That is, they reflect values that cannot be labeled irrational, emotive, or noncognitive merely because their logic is not subsumable to the structural or predictive canons of scientific knowledge.

In fact, as Cassirer developed his analysis of the internal logical forms of language, myth, religion, and art in his monumental *Philosophy of Symbolic Forms* (three volumes, 1923-1929), he realized that the symbolic patterns of these areas were fully as rich and as cognitive as the sciences. But their function for man was different. The mind shapes discursive knowledge in common-sense thought and science to fit the maxim of "always and everywhere," whereas the so-called nondiscursive symbolic forms take on quite different canons of logic.

Without going into the particular nuances which Cassirer found in the nondiscursive, we can note that the psychological intentions that were reflected in the logical structures of language, art, or religion, could be expressed by such ascriptions as emotion, perception, sense, and feeling. Yet in each case—whether language, religion, or art—a rich fabric of symbolism was woven around the psychological valence. Their ideational qualities seemed not to suffer at all because they could not be proven by scientific laws or tested against mathematical axioms. Indeed, Christianity or Buddhism, the art of Praxiteles, Renoir, or Rembrandt, the music of Bach or Beethoven—examples of the highest creative achievements of these domains—were incommensurable in their symbolic structure of meaning with each other or with science. Not only were they logically incomparable, but in their function for human thought and expression in culture they were coequal.

The dominance and superiority we presently assign to science are but a temporary prejudice. If one were to examine culture more comparatively, the tenacity of man in defending his religious, ethnic, and linguistic symbolism would be far more evident than his concern for philosophical or scientific truth, or even material advantage. Not only is science thus shorn of its imperious claims of describing an ultimately real universe through a fixed and objective set of beliefs, but it now shares its position in the spectrum of knowledge with man's other domains of symbolic expression.

THE SYMBOLIC NATURE OF MAN

Though Cassirer's primary concern was the status and scope of knowledge, he soon began to probe into its wider considerations. By establishing symbolic knowledge as the keynote in all experience, both in the discursive areas of science and in the nondiscursive forms of myth, art, language, and religion, Cassirer began to recognize in this unity and diversity in knowledge a clue to the nature of man. Man uses knowledge in different ways. Though the emotionality of myth and the sober logic of science result in far different symbolic structures, they have something in common—the conventional status of symbols. The symbols are not imposed by any outside agency, but by man's own inner ideational concerns interacting with his environment.

Is there then a unifying principle that can explain or at least enrich this insight that originally grew out of logical and epistemological considerations? To answer this question, Cassirer examined new facts and theories in different empirical disciplines such as anthropology and evolutionary theory. Thence came the realization, which Susanne Langer also used as a theme in her writings, that man as a symbol-using creature is unique in the world of nature. The striking contrast that confronted Cassirer when he ultimately examined animal thought as compared with human behavior has been well phrased by Langer:

> Every animal mentality therefore, is built upon a primitive semantic; it is the power of learning by trial and error, that certain phenomena in the world are signs of certain others, existing or about to exist; adaptation to environment is its purpose, and hence the measure of its success. The environment may be very narrow, as it is for the mole, whose world is a back yard, or it may be as wide as an eagle's range and as complicated as a monkey's jungle preserve. That depends on the variety of signals a creature can receive, the variety of combination of them to which he can react, the fixity or flexibility of his responses. Obviously if he have very fixed reactions, he cannot adapt himself to a varied transient environment; if he cannot easily combine and integrate several activities, then the occurrence of more than one stimulus at a time will throw him into confusion; if he be poor in sensory organs—deaf or blind, hard shelled or otherwise limited—he cannot receive many signals to begin with.[19]

[19] Susanne Langer, *op. cit.*, p. 30.

Signs and their meanings act on the animal as signals, i.e., as operators for behavioral adjustments. They direct the animal's eyes, ears, and nose toward the sensory source. Signs announce and indicate their presence. One can epitomize the difference in the status of signs, the psychical intentions or purposes to which they are put, between the animal and human universes of meaning by restating Edward Thorndike's comment that man "thinks about things," whereas animals "think things."[20]

This principle of sign usage can be applied to practically all lower forms. However, the line dividing man from certain species of higher apes is a tenuous one. In the higher apes, the rigid fixity to practically oriented signals is greatly relaxed, while the level of discriminatory behavior is heightened, even to the point of exhibiting certain similarities to human forms of behavior. But even with this increase in range and capacity for integrative responses in the simian's native habitat, without the intervention of human experimentation, the activities are typically practical and adaptational.[21]

The picture Cassirer drew concerning human sign (symbol) behavior is completely different. The purpose with which an animal uses a sign indicates that it is a signal for action. It allows for the survival of the creature. To man, Cassirer argued, the sign has a purely conventional meaning. Man imbues the sign with an arbitrary significance. Symbols are created for the purpose of rendering other symbolic constructs more intelligible. Indeed, as Edward Sapir has noted, when the entire realm of linguistic and cultural symbolism is examined, "there is little that touches ground."[22]

Cassirer incorporated this characteristic of human behavior into a generic description of man as *animal symbolicum:*

> Between the receptor system and the effector system, which are found in all animal species, we find in man a third link which

[20] Edward Thorndike, *Animal Intelligence* (New York: Macmillan Company, 1911), p. 19.
[21] See for example, Wolfgang Köhler, *The Mentality of Apes* (London: Paul, Trench and Trubner, 1927); R. M. and A. W. Yerkes, *The Great Apes* (New Haven: Yale University Press, 1929); E. and K. Hayes, "The Cultural Capacity of the Chimpanzee," in *The Non-Human Primates and Human Evolution* (Detroit: Wayne State University Press, 1955), pp. 110-123.
[22] Edward Sapir, in David G. Mandelbaum (ed.), *Selected Writings* (Berkeley: University of California Press, 1949), p. 568.

we may describe as the symbolic system. The new acquisition transforms the whole of human life. As compared with the other animals man lives not merely in a broader reality, he lives so to speak in a new dimension of reality. There is an unmistakable difference between organic reactions and human responses. In the first case a direct and immediate answer is given to an outward stimulus; in the second case the answer is delayed. It is interrupted and retarded by a slow and complicated process of thought. At first sight such a delay may appear to be a very questionable gain. Many philosophers have warned man against this pretended progress. "L'homme qui médite," says Rousseau, "est un animal déprav"; it is not an improvement but a deterioration of human nature to exceed the boundaries of organic life.[23]

Symbols used by man, Langer also noted, serve "to let us develop a characteristic attitude towards objects in absentia, which is called 'thinking of' or 'referring to' what is not here. Signs in this capacity are not symptoms of things, but symbols."[24]

The core of the argument of Cassirer's philosophy of symbolic forms revolves around the uses to which language is put. Language is the center from which symbolic activity flourishes. In the ontogeny of each human being, the initiation of language is the key for entrance into the circle of social life. Language is a conventional creation of man and utilized by him in a manner unique to each social group. It has few qualities that could be compared with the vocalizations of beasts. It is not instinctively given through the genes, nor does it ever evoke a given set of overt physical responses in all members of the species. It is a system of symbols used not necessarily to communicate actions or innate drives and cues, but to evoke understanding and contemplation—albeit through a diverse variety of symbolic forms.

Symbols in the proper sense of that term cannot be reduced to merely signals. Signals and symbols belong to two different universes of discourse—a signal is a part of the physical world of being; a symbol is a part of the human world of meaning. Signals are "operators," symbols are "designators." Signals even when understood and used as such have nevertheless a sort of physical or substantial being; symbols have only a functional value.[25]

[23] Ernst Cassirer, *An Essay on Man* (New York, Doubleday and Company, Inc., 1953), pp. 42-43.
[24] Langer, *op. cit.*, p. 31.
[25] Cassirer, *op. cit.*, p. 51.

The implications of Cassirer's views on human nature are clear. All views of human nature that reduce human behavior and motivations to those of antecedent drives would be rejected. Reductions of behavior to economic motives rooted in man's social organization or biological drives, which supposedly thrust man toward a goal of social or material adaptation, would likewise be discounted. Man's behavior is not determined by these anterior causes, whether they be the socioeconomic determinants of Marx or the biological instincts of Freud. In regard to Freud's reduction of mythic symbolism to the libidinal drive, Cassirer commented as follows: "It is not a very satisfactory explanation of a fact [myth] that has put its indelible mark upon the whole life of mankind to reduce it to a special and single motive [Oedipus myth]. Man's psychical and cultural life is not made of such simple and homogeneous stuff. . . ."[26]

Man has risen beyond the animal state; he has freed himself from the rigidity of instinctive reactions. Being thus freed, he is not impelled to direct his cultural endeavors toward any fixed goals; there are many goals for which man can set his sights. His choices and his values are given by no ontological nature of the universe or man. As opposed to Dewey, Cassirer implied that the function of human intelligence is not adaptational or exclusively problem-solving. Hence the character and quality of the human cultural venture can be analyzed only by an internal examination of what man does with his symbolic capacities, not by a comparison with an external, biologically rigid conception of human nature.

According to Cassirer, if man is to be conceived as having a nature, it must be functional, not substantial or material.

> The philosophy of symbolic forms starts from the presupposition that if there is any definition of man of the nature or "essence" of man, the definition can only be understood as a functional one, not a substantial one. We cannot define man by any inherent principle which constitutes his metaphysical essence, nor can we define him by an inborn faculty or instinct that may be ascertained by empirical observation. Man's outstanding characteristic, his distinguishing mark, is not his metaphysical or physical nature, but his work. It is this work, it is the system of human activities, which define and determine the circle of

[26] Ernst Cassirer, *The Myth of the State* (New York: Doubleday and Company, Inc., 1955), p. 43.

"humanity." Language, myth, religion, art, science, history, are the constituents, the various sectors of this circle.[27]

Cassirer's conclusion is that the human world has broken irrevocably with its organic tradition.[28] Culture was created by man as an intellectual, ideational vision of experience to give symbolic meaning to his life. If we wish, therefore, to understand all of life, the material as well as the ideational, we must view human culture not as a response to an organic need or superficial involvement with matter, but as part of a symbolic, mediated, and conventional world of meanings.

TOWARD PLURALISM

Cassirer's Argument

The world of human reason and action is a unique but not an arbitrary creation. Since man is a product of the evolutionary process, his knowledge will reflect the world that created him and of which he is an integral part. But this world is unknown to him except through the mediation of his sensory organs and those cerebral structures responsible for the organization of sensory data.

Thus man is never in direct communication with any external forms of reality. This does not mean that the knowledge man constructs from this experience is more fallible than if it were imposed by the external world. All knowledge is tested in experience, and the forms of knowledge are being constantly changed by the force of this experience. Heretofore, the belief that any one system of knowing represented the actual structure of the universe made it difficult to correlate philosophical discourse with man's experience.

Examining the products of man's knowledge in society, some thinkers have attributed the products of culture to specific drives such as sexual or economic. Cassirer rejected these

[27] Ernst Cassirer, *An Essay on Man* (New York: Doubleday and Company, Inc., 1953), p. 93.
[28] See Kurt Goldstein's poetic discussion of this problem, inspired to a great extent by Cassirer, *The Organism: A Holistic Approach to Biology* (New York: American Book Co., 1939), esp. pp. 470-474.

conceptions as simplistic reductionisms.[29] Human nature and thought are made of more complex stuff. To characterize man in a general manner, we should think of him as an animal that has transcended the usual biological preoccupations. His concerns are ideational rather than material. Today the great material and technological achievements of society create the belief that man has unlocked the secrets of nature. The proliferation of material goods is viewed as evidence of the conformity of human thought to the conditions of reality and that man is adapting in an increasingly efficient manner to the external world. Cassirer would deny this, and assert that whatever man has created is a product of thought, a response to the desire for the symbolic envisagement of experience. The great importance given to material and technological development in our day is actually a result of certain symbolic choices made, wisely or unwisely, from an unlimited number of possibilities. There is no external, physical imposition of culture.

The fact that man is not determined in his symbolism by any external forces or specific internal direction does not mean that the process of symbolic envisagement is random and structureless. Both Cassirer and Langer stress the fact that all of man's symbolic creations conform to certain rules of organization. They are patterned on the varied structures of his psychic nature.

One can postulate a dual symbolic patterning as between discursive and presentational symbols, as Langer does, or the general tripartite division of logic, religion and art most often employed by Cassirer. The cause of the existence of these capacities and concerns is unknown. It is a mystery that lies deep within the phylogenetic heritage of the species. Of all the animals, man alone can experience the logic of science, the emotive meaning of communal ritual, and the sensual pleasure

[29] The increasing number of books rejecting recent "ratomorphic" psychological and philosophical tendencies is represented by: Floyd Matson, *The Broken Image* (New York: George Braziller, Inc., 1964); Susanne Langer, *Mind: An Essay on Human Feeling* (Baltimore: The Johns Hopkins Press, 1967); Michael Polanyi, *Personal Knowledge* (Chicago: University of Chicago Press, 1958); Arthur Koestler, *The Ghost in the Machine* (New York: Macmillan Company, 1968); Noam Chomsky, *Cartesian Linguistics* (New York: Harper & Row, Publishers, 1966); Lewis Mumford, *The Myth of the Machine* (New York: Harcourt, Brace & World, 1966).

of artistic experience. Yet none of these attitudes involves the reduction of the mind to any specific biological motive.

Thus an unexplained mystery remains in the writings of these symbolic philosophers. While a solution may be important for the future development of the philosophy, it is not crucial to its internal logic, because Langer and Cassirer were careful to frame their philosophies without making claims on the basis of any presumed set of answers to the enigma of human thought. More important to them was the factual evidence for the existence of the special forms of thought. "We are not concerned here with this metaphysical aspect of the problem [man's mental life]. Our objective is a phenomenology of human culture. We must try, therefore, to illustrate and to elucidate the issue by concrete examples taken from man's cultural life." [30]

If there is a bond that unites the various symbolic modes of thought, it is that they are found in all human cultures. But it ought not be thought that because these facets of culture are to be found universally that, as expressions of man's capabilities each gives an equable account of man's possibilities. The concept of cultural relativism and the criteria of environmental adaptation and stasis are not acceptable. Cassirer found clear evidence in every symbolic area of expression of the progressive development, enrichment, and sophistication of thought, whether it be in language structure, patterns of religious belief, or the varied arts. This cultural development, of which technological control of the environment is but one manifestation, seems to demonstrate that progress in civilization is accompanied by man's evolving idealization of his experience. What this means, very simply, is that as man applies more conscious thought to his various spontaneous cultural expressions, he creates an environment around him that increases his self-satisfaction. What man searches for is meaning. He loves to play games, develop rules and strategies, forms, patterns, and abstractions, so that in every sensory or perceptual experience he can find "sense in his sensations."

Thus primitive cultures all over the world, even with the glorious somnolent and languorous qualities of a Tahiti, cannot, using the same criteria, be compared with ancient Athens,

[30] Ernst Cassirer, *An Essay on Man* (New York: Doubleday & Company, Inc., 1953), p. 75

Renaissance Italy, and England, or eighteenth- or nineteenth-century Vienna and Paris. Here philosophy, science, music, painting, gymnastics, literature and a host of other activities were raised to new heights of creative meaning. These eras, with all their abuses of humanity, still represent peaks amongst all the multifarious symbolic possibilities inherent in culture.

Universality and Plurality

Wherever philosophical reason and science confront the material structure of human experience, they generate laws and principles which extend themselves to wider contents and references of experience. The laws of science, whether discovered by Greek, Roman, Parisian monk, or British mathematics professor, are all intelligible everywhere once the differences in expression are overcome. The world of matter and energy, the physical, even the biological and social worlds, as long as we consider their physical dimensions, seem to suffer no difficulties in transferring theory from one culture to another. For example, we have seen this occur in our own day as peoples as diverse as the Russians and Japanese turned the symbolism of science to their own uses.

In addition, science in all its permutations demands that its principles be applicable not only everywhere but for all time. The aim in science is to find one basic theory of nature from which laws in specific areas can be derived. The thrust of knowledge is encompassed in the dream that someday all the realms of physical experience, inorganic matter, energy, organic substance, biological behavior, even social behavior, will be deducible and predictable once the specific parameters within the great generalizing theory become known to us.

The biological and social realms are less amenable to generalization due to the variables of their structure and function. In addition, in both evolutionary biology and society we have historical and valuational factors to contend with. Scientific thinkers such as Darwin, Pasteur, Mendel, and Freud are honored for the great theoretical generalizations which introduced order and causality into these disciplines heretofore supported only by fragmentary observational principles. The greatness of these men lies not in the success of their universal theories as compared with scientific paradigms of mathematics and physics, but in their enterprise. For certainly the disciplines they represent are still incomplete both in internal logical structure as well as predictability.

The important factor to remember is that man has a drive to unify knowledge and that he applies it equally to all areas of experience. Some disciplines are more tractable than others in this respect. Physics, for example, has fewer variables than the social concepts of human equality and freedom. But the search is the same. Wherever man discovers a new principle of equality with regard to his physical person or his right of personal expression, he attempts to obtain these rights. His search to bring law into the realm of social relations, even to the creation of a United Nations is part of this continuing drive.

Perhaps man will not realize his dream to encompass the physical dimension of all human experience—inorganic, organic, and cultural—within one universal set of principles. Einstein was sadly disappointed in his lifelong quest to unite two realms, the macroscopic one of large motions (trains and stars) and the microscopic, within the nucleus of the atom. Yet when we see how man, without completely understanding his own aggressive intellectual determination, so strives in every dimension of culture, we cannot be sure that his reach will exceed his grasp.

In the cultural modes of expression such as religion and art—nondiscursive forms of thought—a different sense of universality should be postulated. Certainly all cultures have some kind of mythic and religious observances. The arts, in the sense of crafts, dance, ritual, music, and decorative expression, also represent a universal dimension of culture. There are as well poetry, story-telling, humor, personality types, patterns of puberty, birth and death rites, etc. It is understandable that men born with the same basic physiological organization, sensory organs, nervous systems, having the same phylogenetic heritage, and in spite of the variations of beneficent and adverse geographic and ecological environments produce the same forms of cultural expression. That they do this implies a similar internal intellectual structure.[31]

The forms of creativity in the nondiscursive areas men-

[31] See Noam Chomsky's review of B. F. Skinner's "Verbal Behavior" *Language* (January-March 1959), pp. 26-58; also Noam Chomsky, *Cartesian Linguistics* (New York: Harper and Row, Publishers, 1966).

tioned above may be the same, but in meaning they do not spread out to wider logical reference in experience and thus do not communicate to men of different cultures. True, in myth and religion we note certain universal emotional themes—the sacred and the profane, awe and humility, the bond of sympathy with life and nature and the awareness of an ultimate beyond man. Yet the concrete religious patterns for each people are unique and untranslatable. This is appropriate, for these patterns are built up from the interpersonal relationships that groups share over a long period of time. The symbols have thus absorbed the meanings of the various communal events of past history. The diverse accoutrements of ritual, the prayers, the artifacts, the holy shrine, must all remain unique to the internal experiences of the culture.

Art tends to become fixed in a pluralistic locus also. True, in its material envisagement, in the cups and plates of antiquity and prehistory, in the jewelry and even in architecture there can be similarities. In music, in literature, the possibility of wider meaning, however, becomes especially delimited. (Aggressor peoples usually steal the artifacts, but burn the manuscripts.) Even among our Western nations, how difficult it is to render literary works from their original language without destroying the intimate flavors of the original. "In art we are absorbed in their immediate appearance, and we enjoy this appearance to the fullest extent in all its richness and variety. Here we are not concerned with the uniformity of laws but with the multiformity and diversity of intention."[32]

In the sciences, logic demands that each local difference be related in theory to a larger law. In science, difference is symbolically noted, so that it can be eliminated. On the other hand, to the extent that they unite a unique community, cultural differences in religion and art are reinforced. They serve to signify to the participants a special shared set of symbolic experiences. The fixed structure of material experience with which science is concerned and which conditions the universal trend of theory and the concomitant capacity of science to generalize is irrelevant and meaningless in the nondiscursive realm.

Therefore, the natural mode of cultural expression here

[32] Cassirer, *op. cit.*, p. 216.

tends towards the more plural forms. History supports the conclusion that, given uncoerced conditions of social life, natural communities will always be formed within which each will display its own linguistic accents and dialects, artistic styles, and social customs—in short, all those shared nuances of cultural life by which life is made worthwhile.

It is important to note that while the pluralistic characteristic in culture is intrinsic, this does not mean that social life is predestined to fragmentation or that it is incapable of absorbing the universalist qualities of discursive thought. The ideal of social equality and the international assent given to us today in the principles of the United Nations—and which have existed as an ideal of Western man since the Stoics—suggest that scientific canons of thought can be applied to the external relationships between men. Merely to ask the question *Are men equal?* is to realize that universal reason must be applicable to the social domain as it is to the physical.

The difference between discursive and nondiscursive thought, as well as their cultural realizations in respect to universality and plurality, has yet to be explained. One need only examine the contemporary character of symbolic thought, however, to realize that this theory merely reflects the rank commonalities of human experience. Culture is a curious admixture of unities and pluralities integrated into the fabric of social life. The answer to the mystery of the one and the many lies somewhere in the nature of man's symbolic powers. Whatever the resolution to these problems, we may assume that this dual quality in human existence—the universal and plural—will be manifested both increasingly and more self-consciously.

The Irrational

Though man's drive to direct his perceptual experience into the symbolic patterns, consonant with the steady direction of reason, will continue in the future as it has in the past, it will not necessarily take place smoothly or without regression. When man confuses his psychic interests and when reason loses its guiding power, havoc is likely to ensure, as Cassirer argued in *The Myth of the State.* This book grew out of the experience of Nazi Germany, where there was a premeditated desire to destroy the secular power of reason by attacking the rational and scientific use of language. Language, being a flexible tool available to the scientific, mythic, ánd esthetic symbolic modes, was easily diverted. By controlling education, the press, and other sources of rational usage to pervert the German language for mythic purposes, the Nazis hoped to destroy the power of their opponents. Word meanings were changed to conjure up new images.

The attack went beyond language to all the heretofore rational institutions of society. These were gradually subverted to the point that men could no longer think or act logically on the basis of experience. Their precarious politicial and economic situation stimulated a wave of mythic passions that paralyzed discursive thought.

> The men who coined these terms [*Siegfried* for *Sieger-friede*] were masters of the art of political propaganda. They attained their end, the stirring up of violent political passions by the simplest means. A word, or even the change of a syllable in a word, was often good enough to serve this purpose. If we hear these new words we feel in them the whole gamut of human emotions—of hatred, anger, fury, haughtiness, contempt, arrogance and disdain.[33]

For the Nazis to attain their ends, it was also necessary to destroy the older symbolic rituals and religious forms. In this case the Jews were chosen, because, according to Cassirer, they represented a humane conception of religion. Also, persecution of the Jews was a means to unite the masses under the new myths. Thus, by extending a more primitive mythic symbolism into every previously secular area of activity, all powers of judgment were lulled and reason was eliminated as a force.

Philosophical Reason

Man alone amongst the animals has the capacity to act out many moods—joy, religious ecstasy, analytical thought, foolishness—and at the same time know that he is so engaged. He can at once break off and resume another set of attitudes. The rules, the mores, and folkways of tradition have usually guided man to his appropriate habits in primitive cultures. The Greeks made a great new discovery regarding these varied

[33] Ernst Cassirer, *The Myth of the State* (New York: Doubleday and Company, Inc., 1955), p. 357.

dimensions of human behavior—philosophy. It was a manifestation of man's capacity to stand aside from his prejudices and
examine himself and nature dispassionately. This eventually enabled man to guide cultural evolution, to bind it to his will.

The closest ally of philosophical intelligence is education. In
the course of one generation we have the capacity to refine and
reshape the attitudes and understanding of the young in accor-
dance with an advanced state of philosophical understanding.
As Dewey often pointed out, every philosophy is in a sense its
own complete educational system having content and method
implicit, in the richest valuational sense.

The use of reason as a tool for reshaping attitudes and institutions in a society is a crucial yet delicate issue. What was
achieved so late in human history, lost and rediscovered again
and again, is a dimension of man that is not permanently attained in any one historical stage of development. Its achievement depends on man's constant struggle to retain intellectual
control over the complexities of his social life. For the philosophic quality of mind to be stimulated, an articulated structure
of ideas must be available. This usually consists of the traditional dimensions of philosophy—ethics, ontology, logic, and a
theory of human nature. It is enough here to note that philosophy is generated from the same sober attitudes of discursive
thought we usually invoke in science, except that it is the most
general or universal of intellectual forms. That it transcends the
purely material concerns of science to go into questions of social value, art, religion, is evidence enough of its intellectual
priority.

CONCLUSION

In the philosophical argument developed in this chapter we
have attempted to lay the foundation for our claim that human
nature and knowledge are more complex than usually assumed
in the social and cultural orientation that dominates our mass
society. An attempt has also been made to surmount the limitations in the understanding of man and society inherent in
Dewey's adaptational and problem-solving approach. Man is a
creature with richer and more complex motivations than the
pragmatic interpretation gave us reason to believe. Religion, for

example, in our view, has a deeper and more fundamental function in all of human culture than as a means of facilitating social cohesion and unity of practical purposes, as ascribed by Dewey in *a Common Faith.* Religion in its reflection of the peculiar abiological condition of man, of man's unique aloneness and need for commitment to values that both free and limit his actions, will exist when the present churches are gone. It is likewise unreasonable to believe that there is no function for religion outside the explicit regulation of our discursive social and ethical behavior—aspects such as divorce and population control.

Horace Kallen was correct when he hypothesized that cultural pluralism was deeply rooted in man as an intrinsic need and value. But he was perhaps mistaken in supposing that it would go underground when attacked by the existing undemocratic institutional framework of society. To go underground and resist, pluralism would have needed stronger philosophical support for the implicit beliefs of the various ethnic minorities. This was not forthcoming, and the pressures of succeeding events effected a greater measure of assimilation than would have been expected at that time.

In one important sense, pluralism did go underground. To the extent that the diversity in our cultural life has been diminished, that there are few viable intermediate institutions between the solitary individual and the state, that communities have been cauterized in fulfilling their manifold cultural functions for man—to this extent an underground has been created. It has, however, manifested itself in a more subtle rebellion, that of a cancerous psychosocial growth gradually enveloping and debilitating our materialistic mass society. While the organizational structure and its hucksters stake their claims for legitimacy on the satisfactions of basic human needs in the artifacts that pour so efficiently from the industrial centers, the deeper denial of important human rights gradually takes its social toll.

There will be no hope for peace through revision and reform of this society until we begin to plan for a more natural set of cultural dynamics. But to achieve this we must educate men to their own wants and to the possibility of making rational choices. The philosophy of cultural pluralism is not obsolete merely because the immigrant groups of an earlier generation are for the most part absorbed; pluralism in culture arises from too fundamental a set of human needs. It is as natural to man as are science and technology. Thus it will eventually be manifested.

Let us now shift the argument to the social context to inquire into this problem of the rational apportionment of human thought and action in its proper symbolic expression. The question is not alone "Whether or not pluralism?" but Where ought the various discursive and nondiscursive attitudes inherent in thought apply to achieve a more substantive vision of the good life?

chapter 4

Pluralism in Democracy

CULTURE: A FUNDAMENTAL DUALISM

The social conditions that have fostered pluralistic forms of behavior until recently have now been largely displaced by a new set of dynamics. But this does not mean that pluralism is obsolete, not if we argue that the plural dimension of thought and knowledge is intrinsic to man. Man is far more complex than the social patterns of today may reflect. The emphasis has been increasingly on the discursive areas of knowledge—science, technology, politics, and economics. The results have led inevitably toward universality in thought and uniformity in quality.

Of course we value the more intimate dimensions of cultural expression. But we have expected they would endure without our planning for them amid our more external experience. On occasion we have even heard civic groups argue against music and art in our schools because they are "frills." The cult of rationality which has ascribed importance only to our more discursive scientific forms of logical thought, has tended by its denigration of the nondiscursive areas to exclude them from consideration in our social planning. But these areas of culture are not irrational. They are not unstructured or chaotic in form. However, they do serve a different psychological purpose for man. They serve to order his perceptual and emotional experiences in a taut and resilient, if largely invisible web of cultural meanings.

The distinction between science and art then is not one of order against chaos or prediction versus intuition, but rather one of psychological attitudes. Discursive knowledge is a product of thought; it represents the satisfaction of a psychological tendency in man to encompass experience in terms of universal symbols. Science and logical thought seek to answer all questions to assure their validity everywhere, always, and for everyone. Not only does this tendency express itself in the material world; it is equally observable in the biological and social domains. Scientific thought, indeed, uses the various areas of experience, including the material, to rise beyond the sensory image—the particular experiential regularity—to construct theories of greater abstractness, ideality, and generality.[1]

On the other hand, in many cultural areas the goal of thought is not to rise beyond the particular, or to see every special instance as part of a more universal regularity. Here thought is satisfied with the particular, the unique flavor, or experience.[2] Let us take language for an example. True, languages themselves have a formal structure. They have been shown to evolve and drift phonetically in a manner that is regular, at times even subject to predictive canons. Language orders and regulates ordinary common-sense behavior; it is used at the same time as a means of philosophic expression. But it has even broader possibilities. It can communicate subtle nuances of meaning not capable of being translated from one language to another. Language is also literature, poetry, humor, intimacy. These dimensions can exist only within communities of understanding. Such diversity becomes irrelevant when we think of communities in terms of universal conditions. The "community of mankind" thus becomes an abstraction within which the intimate and particulate are dessicated and die.

One can better appreciate the distinction we have been making with regard to these modalities of thought by considering from a historic perspective our attitudes toward man's creations. Science advances by supplementation and displacement. Thus we do not think of Galilean and Newtonian science as having merely enriched Aristotelian and Ptolemaic forms. Neither do we see Einstein's theories as merely a more general form of Newtonian mechanics. If we utilize mechanical theory today it is because in our domain of macroscopic entities and slower speeds the errors from Einstein's principles are insignifi-

[1] Emile Meyerson, *Identity and Reality* (London: George Allen and Unwin, 1929).
[2] J. A. Talmon, *The Unique and the Universal* (London: Secker and Warburg, 1965).

cant. Practically speaking, Newtonian calculations are acceptable. From the standpoint of logical deduction, mechanical theory is not a special case of relativity theory. Also, Darwinian evolutionary theory is not merely to be considered alongside Buffon, Lamarck, or Agassiz. The basic assumption of each successive scientific development is to be thought of as replacing other basic a priori views.

On the other hand not only cross-culturally but within cultures, the nondiscursive is valued cumulatively. When in rebuilding our cities it becomes necessary to raze structures, even if for good rational reasons—in terms of engineering they are obsolete, in terms of economics, unremunerative—there will be cries to save the old. Not for material but for historical or esthetic reasons the old is still of worth. From one standpoint, the Acropolis or Roman Forum may be merely a pile of rubble!

Although we can compare technology or science or economics in terms of progress and truth, can we compare one literature with another? Can we compare French, English, and Russian novelists, using a universal criterion for excellence? Can we even do so within a cross section of one nation, say Chaucer, Shakespeare, and Keats? Such comparisons in terms of esthetic displacement are patently meaningless. Each nation adds to the other's culture in spatial as well as in temporal terms. We can establish international standards to judge which society has built the largest building, has the most death-dealing weapons or has designed the fastest form of land transport. But one does not even attempt to make judgments about the finest national cuisine, most beautiful apparel styles, or the richest folk music traditions. Which religion is the most ideational, warmest and most comforting—Hinduism, Islam, or Christianity? The world is certainly better to the extent that men do not ask such questions for which there are no logical canons of agreement.

The natural reaction of intelligent opinion is to cherish these wide cultural differences. Side by side they do not distract from each other, even as mutually unintelligible to each other as might be Tagalog and Ukranian. No national language or esthetic strives for universal domination or truth. Each does have priority, but only in the internal cultural context in which participants can share their meanings.

Science and technology are bringing men closer together in

theory and practice. The nondiscursive dimensions of culture are testimony to the fact that man has created areas of meaning that are intrinsic and self-satisfying. Each voluntary community therefore shares with its fellows in the community of mankind certain basic universal interests and concerns and at the same time succors each man's special purview of meaning. Uncoerced, man will create out of this natural, universal, and pluralistic set of circumstances a cohesive and enhancing fabric of social existence.

THE PROBLEM OF DEMOCRACY

Form and Substance

We educate our young for life in a democracy. Our school curricula are suffused with democratic value commitments. We have a written body of law brought into being by popularly elected legislators. The executive division of our government, also popularly elected, carries out, enforces, and administers the law. The validity of their actions is checked by constitutional restraints and procedures, due process is assured, and the most fundamental if unstated human rights are succored, all by an independent judiciary. Finally, we cherish the checks and balances, the countervailing powers that interpenetrate the whole process of government so as to frustrate any untoward thrust for dominance from any one part.

We preach obedience to law to our young. On occasion, and at least in theory, we support the right of dissent. Our democratic commitment is supposedly fulfilled by our appearance at the polling place to exercise the franchise. Yet there has been a realization in recent times that the formalism in democratic procedures is significant only to the extent that substantive issues are also subject to the democratic process. This is akin to the belated realization of the need for the protection of individual liberties, covered in the Bill of Rights by our founding fathers.

It is quite possible to have all the procedures of democracy yet at the same time to arrange the content of an educational system, the communication media, and all of the well-ordered institutions of our mass society so that the basic intent of democracy is nullified. Every recent totalitarian state has prided itself on its cultivation of the formal apparatus and documents of a democracy. It is obvious that without more substantive evidence the democratic life is a hoax.

The political option of democracy has always appeared to be the likeliest means of advancing not only the interests of the many but also raising the level of intelligence. The processes of democracy have always been thought to be the best means of insuring the good life. The essence of democracy is thus not fulfilled in the act of voting. Without tangible discussions of the subject matter of social existence, no set of abstract protections will ever by sufficient. Otherwise the draft-card burners, the religious dissidents, the polygamists and peyote smokers will be at the mercy of the vigilantes who are eager to extirpate any hint of dissent or difference.

Democracy, then, has to have a content. It has to be a place where the most diverse set of arguments contribute to the shaping of the qualitative dimension of human life. The protection of minorities can take place only where there is philosophical discussion, overt and explicit. It is when the tacit philosophical claims of the majority are covert, overlaid by assumed social conventions, that the judiciary will find it convenient to avoid its responsibility for making the decisions of what kinds of liberties and exclusions are going to be retained by our inevitable minorities.[3]

At the beginning of our own democratic history, while the machinery—the Constitution and the Bill of Rights, for example—existed that was crucial to the construction of our nation, there also existed an impelling philosophy of human nature and society. This philosophy represented the almost universally accepted educated opinion of that time and as such received little explicit delineation. Thus from the Newtonian scientific philosophy of physical bodies in motion our leaders derived the values of political, economic, and intellectual freedom epitomized in the writings of John Locke, Adam Smith, and our own leaders, Franklin, Jefferson, and Madison.[4] The idea of the diminished state and the freedom of the individual

[3] Harold Laski, *Foundations of Sovereignty* (New York: Harcourt, Brace & World, 1921), pp. 28-29.
[4] J. Bronowski and Bruce Mazlish, *The Western Intellectual Tradition* (New York: Harper & Row, Publishers, 1960). See chapters on each of these men.

to pursue his conscience in the realm of ideas or commerce were the natural consequence of a view of the universe whose laws of motion applied to man as well as to matter. The free movement of matter, both celestial and terrestrial, had produced an orderly structured and rational world of which man was an integral part. The harmonizing of the varied actions taken freely by rational men (what Isaiah Berlin has described as the *volonté de tous*) was assumed from this belief.[5]

But the twentieth century is far more complex than the laissez-faire society of the eighteenth. The opportunities and openness of that era led to the assumption of certain intrinsic and absolute rights which today are inimical to society. We were disillusioned more than once with such simple philosophical perspectives. If we are to achieve more than the veneer of the democratic life, we need to redefine nature and knowledge, both physical and human.

Dewey and Cassirer

So that we may better appreciate the potentialities of the symbolic hypothesis, let us again note Dewey's approach to the philosophy of democracy. One of his greatest achievements was to underline the importance of a substantive view of the democratic life.[6] Dewey's vision of man in nature and society grew out of the intellectual ferment of the post-Darwinian epoch, 1875-1920.

According to Dewey's modification of Darwinian evolutionary teachings, man could not be reduced to the animal level, even though he was a creation of evolution.[7] Thus, as we have previously noted, Dewey postulated a generalized trichotomization of human nature—impulse, habit, and intelligence—which achieved its most elaborate exposition in *Human Nature and Conduct*. Dewey maintained that intelligence is a natural capacity in man that is largely latent in the course of historical

[5] Isaiah Berlin, *Karl Marx* (New York: Oxford Galaxy, 1959), pp. 35–44.

[6] Morton White, *Social Thought in America* (Boston: Beacon Press, 1957).

[7] John Dewey, *Human Nature and Conduct* (New York: Henry Holt & Co., 1922), p. 131. Cassirer extensively and approvingly quotes Dewey on this matter in *An Essay on Man* (New York: Doubleday & Company, Inc., 1962), p. 67.

evolution. It is only gradually recognized and utilized. Only when man discovers that intelligence can free him from biological impulse and social habit can he begin to realize the capacities inherent in his biosocial makeup. For Dewey creative and instrumental thought, when used appropriately by man, is the most significant organ of human adaptation.

Like Dewey, Cassirer viewed the utilization of scientific intelligence in human culture as a gradual process. They disagreed, however, on the use of intelligence. To Cassirer, the natural use of intelligence was not to adjudicate between biological and social demands, as it was to Dewey. Cassirer's treatment of the biological aspects of human behavior turned what Dewey defined as "impulse" into the emotionality of the mythic mind.[8] If we follow Cassirer, we can never reduce any of man's activities to biological forces. According to Cassirer, all human activity is governed by some symbolic need of envisagement. Mythic action is never raw, undifferentiated vitality. It is always a vitality guided toward some symbolic reference. Whether it is terror, joy, a sense of the holy or the taboo, or even the warmth and sympathy of social communion, it will have tangible form and structure.

Primitive man's earliest confusions of fact and fancy have been gradually reconstructed into a stable and logical discursive structure of ideas useful in orienting common-sense behavior. To Cassirer, scientific intelligence is a conscious means of bringing order and structure to man's experience. Thus, through the symbolic power of science, the world becomes a more intelligible entity. The problems that man can attack through the sciences do potentially enable him to resolve his social life in an orderly and peaceful manner. However, the prime purpose of science in this resolution is not merely the biological survival of man, but the satisfaction of his restless search for meaning.

This difference between Dewey and Cassirer in their metaphysics of human nature is important to an evaluation of society and therefore of the concept of democracy. Ours is a changing universe. And, according to Dewey, the basic function of an organized society should be to effect the resulting social

---

[8] Susanne Langer, "On Cassirer's Theory of Language and Myth," in Paul A. Schilpp (ed.), *The Philosophy of Ernst Cassirer* (New York: Tudor Publishing Co., 1949), pp. 379-400.

change in the most peaceable manner possible. To Dewey, the fear of any absolutistic and deterministic vision of society necessitated that we keep our vistas forever open to change. Individuality must be given an unfettered opportunity to manifest itself. Science should be utilized as a tool in education to protect this evolving social democracy by resolving the inevitable disturbances of a dynamic changing world.

Dewey advised that a pluralistic society would facilitate a freer environment for personal individuality. It would liberate men from encrusted customs and archaic institutions. Pluralism should therefore facilitate experimental intelligence. In the final Deweyan analysis, social and personal individualism became instrumentalities serving the higher order of natural evolution.

Deweyan Democracy Criticized

Deweyan democracy in effect creates a rudderless ship of state. The voyage is the important thing. The ship must be navigated smoothly, all problems must be overcome democratically. It has neither specific ports of call nor destiny. We cannot tell whether any seemingly illogical short-term decisions, which might result in long-term gains for society, would be preferred over immediate results, which could only temporarily further the democratic values of the society. We could ask whether the apparent equality that comes from subsuming all parts of our culture to one set of values, rewards, and actions would lead eventually to an enrichment of individuality. Or we could inquire whether an integrated society, though it establishes certain tangible and *prima facie* symbols of equality and democracy for the immediate future, would ultimately result in the negation of freedom and individuality. As Horace Kallen and I. B. Berkson have suggested, the assimilation that was accepted by our immigrants, though offered in a philanthropic and humanitarian spirit, has left our nation more improverished culturally and therefore less free.

Dewey's view of democracy is, therefore, bereft of a vision of a human nature with real criteria upon which we might model our social structure. In spite of Dewey's attempts to the contrary, his views still reinforce an externalized structural approach to the democratic life. There is an historical emptiness in a view purporting only to place individuality at the service of social change. Unless we know the character and form of this change, whether it is economic, political, or social, we cannot establish valid criteria for decision making. Man, in order to progress in his quest for freedom, must have at least tentative standards or goals against which to measure his contemporary success or failure.

THE UNIVERSAL IN SOCIAL THOUGHT

Our view of democracy must harmonize with the previously delineated interpretation of human thought. Both concepts—the symbolic position of human nature and the dual tendencies of knowledge—have to support our interpretation of democracy. Our focus turns to society, and our approach is to see in society a developing exemplification of the direction of thought.

This is hardly the commonly accepted opinion of the matter. Society is usually interpreted as a product of man's adaptation to nature. Thus the various patterns of social living in each culture are a direct consequence of man's need to make a living. After all, Eskimos do live in igloos and wear seal fur, the Congolese live in grass huts and pick fruit from trees. The character of man's response is in direct relation to the adaptive need. What man does merely reflects a reaction required of all organic forms.

Not only is this position inaccurate in its basic assumptions about man's adaptive status in the world, but it is superficial as well. True, man uses his environment to fulfill the biological requirements of life—food and shelter. But man is hardly passive with regard to the conditions of life as he finds them. History testifies to the contrary.

Man, along with several closely related hominoid forms, came into roughly the same world that countless other biological forms inherited. Yet shortly after his arrival his powerful innovative nature alone had transformed the environment around him. The scope, richness, and diversity of his creations came from potentialities within. The environment was the means toward the end of symbolic envisionment.

It is thus plausible to assume that the same cognitive trend exemplified in the various physical and biological domains of experience can be found in social evolution. And if the vector of rational thought in these former areas is the principle of universal entailment, then it is likely that in the social areas, the search for principles and regularities of this sort can likewise be noted. "Universality is not a term which designates a certain field of thought, it is an expression of the very character of the function of thought. Thought is always universal."[9]

The social world is incomparably more complex than the physical and thus provides many more difficulties for the intellect. As a result social thinkers have tended to take their models of thought from the inevitably simpler schematisms of physics and biology rather than from the intrinsic materials of society.[10] The social Darwinists used biological models; the thought of John Locke and Benjamin Franklin reflected Newtonian and mechanical archetypes. Further back we can recall the influence of Aristotle's biological theories for the medievalists, the use of Heraclitean fire and Empedocles' four elements by the Stoics, the atomism of the Epicureans from Leucippus and Democritus, and even Plato's fascination with Pythagorean number mysticism (in the *Republic*).

Man wants to find meaning in his social world. He believes that reason can transform the chaos of experience into order. In fact, he has to believe it, for the search is one with his basic organic structure. He therefore finds his analogies where he can, in the stars, in number, atoms or in the vital actions of other living creatures. Even before the onset of philosophical thought and the beginning of man's ability to articulate consciously his questions about himself, the process of intellectualization was occurring. In primitive and preliterate societies, patterns of ritualization, social stratification, and totemism all reflect the as yet inchoate desire to understand, to order and universalize experience. The history of intellectual thought, however, exemplifies the fact that generally one all-powerful philosophical *leitmotif* dominates, physics having had usual priority, being subsequently and analogically applied to other domains. This can be seen in the influence of the mechanical model on such supposedly independent areas as genetics (the granular character of

---

[9] Ernst Cassirer, *An Essay on Man* (New Haven: Yale University Press, 1962), p. 186.

[10] To extricate theorists from this necessity, Leslie White has founded a "culturological" tradition free of biological or physics overtones. See *The Science of Culture* (New York: Grove Press, Inc., 1949).

the gene) and psychology (the methodological physicalism of Clark Hull).

Equality

Change and diversity in nature have challenged the theoretical mind since the Milesian Greek, Thales, in the sixth century B.C., for the logical demand of thought is for permanence, unity, and order. It is this dialectic between raw sensory experience and the inner integrative demands of mind that has provided the impetus for physical theory ever since.

So, too, in the social realm, a disequilibrium has existed between what men have experienced as the facts of their social existence and the life which they sometimes only inchoately dreamed of creating. The world of stratification, of inequality, of exploitation was an even more difficult set of social circumstances to accept than the world of changing sensory phenomena which the physical theorist confronted. The physical theorist could only be troubled intellectually by the chaotic world that he wanted to order and systematize.

The ideal of equality dreamed of by men, however, derived from certain overt perceptual facts. Man was made strongly aware of these facts every time he was subjected to the interpersonal indignities of the existing environment. In this sense, equality was a perception searching for symbolic envisagement—theory—and which could not be explained away by any social status quo. Both exploiters and exploited were held in a bond of relatedness whereby they could realize their equality in mortal birth and death, in the weaknesses and temporality of the flesh. Even as committed a Greek as Aristotle could enunciate the humanity of non-Greeks, and thus "barbarians" and the conventionality of slavery. Yes, even the masters might be by nature of slavish character. And who is to argue that the social dynamics of history are not impelled by this disequilibrium between perception and reality in which the perception of "humanity" perennially searches for a theoretical envisagement which will legitimatize these dangerous thoughts?

We can hardly doubt, then, that what few achievements in human dignity and freedom we have gained have benefited from an intrinsic cognitive drive of man to bring about the substance of what his raw perception must tell him: viz., that the exploitation and subjugation of man by man is not chartered in the nature of things. To each enunciation of the vision of equality and justice through the various philosophies of Stoicism, Buddhism, Christianity, and Marxism, man has responded powerfully, giving evidence of a universal susceptibility to this aspiration.

But as strong as this steady insistence is, its possibility of seriously weakening the various power structures is limited. For as Marx has shown, each new exploiter class not only dissolves the power forms of the previous exploiters but also develops new and subtler philosophic rationales for its own inegalitarianism. It is not enough solely to feel strongly that one has rights equal to others. Throughout history men have been subject to abuse and exploitation while patiently awaiting the philosophical promulgation of new and revolutionary egalitarian ideals. The armament of reason is necessary to strike down the status quo.

As we have become philosophically aware that forms of social relations under which men live are mere conventions and are not rooted in any eternal metaphysical order of things, it has grown increasingly difficult to rationalize the grosser inequalities and exploitations. But to translate the awareness by man of an abstract egalitarian moral and social ideal into a concrete social reality remains as difficult as ever. Our contextual problems—equality of opportunity, differential rewards for varying social contributions, the right of individual enterprise and its social responsibility, welfare protection, social progress versus traditions—all these contribute to the blurring of this ideal.

The opaque meaning of equality and freedom in our time testifies to the current tangle of problems and perplexities. For it is when a great social tradition loses its inertial impetus, begins to generate antithetical movements, and stumbles to a halt, that the lack of clarity of vision is either cause or consequence. Our intellectual troughs coincide with our social derelictions. Thus today the moral and intellectual domains, weak and flaccid, are playing second fiddle to technological priorities, which themselves have little élan.

We are now in the later phases of a society produced by the mechanical world view. As noted earlier, this interpretation of man in terms of his particulate individuality has precipitated a polarization between the state and the defenseless, often alienated, individual being. The mechanical world view made us aware of many rights not heretofore honored in social life, while sterilizing a portion of our social life—the communitarian and cultural—that is a traditional part of man's millieu. The cause is not ill intent but intellectual myopia.

If the world of physics has shifted in its focus upon such varied concepts as matter, energy, light, and quantum in the continuing effort to unify this realm of experience, the social world has presented, at least on the surface, a more self-evident focus for these quasi-physicalist attitudes—individual man. It is man who constitutes nations, armies, clubs, totems, teams, tribes, communities. Social theories cannot further divide him into molecules or physiological functions, nor can man's social organizations ever be realistically seen as enveloping his individual will in a larger totality. Men have been spoken of as children of God, participants in the evolution of the *Weltgeist*, endowed with certain inalienable rights, members of a classless society. Regardless of the fact that these larger conceptual relations on occasion tended to clarify thought, we are, according to this argument, forever drawn back to the unassailable particularity, distinctiveness, and irreducibility of individual man, the fact of the independence of his will and his potentiality for action. Because of this, all attempts at lawmaking in the social realm have recently been directed, even if obliquely, at the necessity for rationalizing the relations between individual men.

All the social laws and the concomitant social revolutions of history have implicitly evoked man's rational capacities. They have assumed his ability to seek out cause and effect, structural principles by which organizational concepts are formed, the whole and its parts, the particular and the general idea, and finally to discover that behind the social façade of the supposed inequalities in men that have been paraded through history, men are inherently equal and valuable.

Men are made of the same stuff, are destined for the same cycles of birth and death, love and hate, happiness and tragedy. This universality of thought expressed in social law is not one that demands sameness for all of man's actions, or claims that talent and weakness are uniformly distributed. Men need not share the same symbols of language, religion, and culture to be worthy of human treatment. The principle of universal equality implies only that the external relations between men be devoid of the coercive element of power—that one or more individuals may not control the destinies and choices of others without the specific and freely delegated use of power. One of the primary concerns of a democratic society is the unending search for hidden and illegitimate uses of power. Where such corrupting conditions do exist, we can with fairness claim that an irrational social structure has come into being and awaits rationalization by those subject to it.

That there is a universal law at work that seeks to establish a principle of equality between men is more than an assertion deduced from the realm of epistemology and, circuitously, physical theory. True, this form of logical deduction might in itself lend the argument a certain plausibility. But more than that, it is a principle that clarifies the dynamics of social history. It seems to support the assumption of human rationality and the possibility for ameliorating suffering and the overall enhancement of human existence.

THE PROBLEM OF CULTURAL PLURALISM

The Right of Culture

The power of scientific reason and technology has in the last three centuries destroyed most of the vestiges of traditional Western society. Science has promised man much. It has created conditions whereby he could be freed of the ancient and artificial privileges of kings and queens, priests, lords, and feudal barons. No matter that new hierarchies of privilege have been created. Reason can now detect and eventually destroy them too. Man has discovered with great exhilaration that he is not to be laden by brute labor or by physical exploitation for the benefit of a small privileged class. His confidence is buttressed by the awareness that reason, science, and technology can prevent physical deprivation.

As a result of these miraculous gifts he has assented to the social arrangements that have accompanied science and technology. The world has thus become more neutral qualitatively. The organizational arrangements in politics, economics, militarism, and technology which have become necessary as an outgrowth of science have given values a quantitative character.[11] Man has accepted these eventualities because they are presumed to be a necessary prelude to the good life. Has he not repeatedly heard that man must have bread before he can enjoy Bach? But somehow the necessary prelude has never been successfully fulfilled. Man's attentions became exhausted in the material dimensions of experience; he has had little energy for focusing on the more substantive rewards of our new society.

The transformation of individual rights in the last several centuries has duplicated the above economic situation. These liberties represent an enormous step forward as compared to the precarious state of individual existence prior to the modern era. But they have been purchased at a price, the dimensions of which we are today just beginning to perceive. Every extension of individual liberty has encompassed man more tightly in the structure of our mass system. The world is ever more egalitarian. Now all of us can *equally* commit our allegiance to the economic, military, and political forms that support the existing order. In our "individualism," we can choose between General Motors or Ford for our autos, we can work for the Rockefeller Foundation, IBM, or the University of California, we can vote for the Democratic or Republican parties.

Modern industrial man may be relatively wealthy or secure economically, but who is he? The Protestant, Catholic, and Jew are unidentifiable.[12] The character of life, the values, thoughts, and art of the nation are the same, whether one lives in Oregon or Maine. Always more regulated by national licensing, from education to religion, man's vaunted independence is increasingly spurious. Without that deepest sense of autonomy that comes from the emotional and mental freedom given in the possibility of choice, man can only be half-formed. The traditional society at least provided a measure of intimacy, independence, and integrity. If we did not like life, we could go elsewhere and start anew. Where can we go today? We have rejected our former ethnic and cultural values because we have been told

[11] Richard Lichtman, "Towards Community," Center for the Study of Democratic Institutions, Santa Barbara, 1966.
[12] Will Herberg, *Protestant, Catholic, Jew* (New York: Doubleday & Company, Inc., 1955).

that they are products of authoritarian political, social, and philosophical traditions. This argument is more apparent than real. But who can take the time to evaluate the issue? We have accepted as the price of democracy, equality, and liberty supreme loyalty to the modern technological society. On with the new!

But what are the cultural rights that men surrender? They represent an intimate inexpressible dimension of experience; therefore, they are difficult to speak about discursively. How does one blueprint such things as the nature of friendships, the kinds of human associations that are possible within a cultural community as contrasted with those of the public world. Formalities are at a minimum within a culture. Men are not on guard to give only the proper cues, the right appearance, word or gesture. These flow naturally from the very "isness" of the person. The rules for acceptance have been learned from the day of birth, so the intimacy is easy and secure. Status also becomes irrelevant; the satisfactions of social occasions are intrinsic. Warmth and intimacy grow out of the recognition of circumstances greater than a man's mere external vocational achievements. The enjoyment of the person is concrete and specific to the person, not honorific or official. An entire series of expressive nuances flow easily—humor, camaraderie, flirtation, family affection and discipline, even argumentation and bickering. Friends seek each other out so that they can share these essential values that constitute an oasis from the external struggle for economic and material survival.

Here men take pleasure in infusing significance into the most prosaic of material things—a song, a few rhymed words, a carved solid object, or an arrangement of colors. This is the beginning of a process that may be fulfilled in public performance, publication, or exhibition in a museum. Language is special in such a context. It is not as precise, grammatical, articulated, or well modulated as in the more public world. On the other hand it is economical, a little serves to communicate. It has melodic nuance; indeed it is the stuff of which song and poetry are made. Art begins in a context where creator, performer, audience, and critic meet face-to-face, and often where roles may be interchanged. The symbols of import have to be shared with others to have meaning. Art occurs when perceptual experience is endowed with some particular emotional connotation and emphasis; therefore, a unique set of shared meanings stands at the source of art. But to conceive that art can be abstracted from the intimate personal sources of informal cultural life to be reproduced in the formal institutional atmosphere of universities, philanthropic "retreats" is a chimera.

For a culture to exist its members must live together, even in a voluntary ghetto. If they live together they can share their history and celebrate the experiences and events of their forebears, in religion, ritual, art, particularly in education and morals. We often think of ethics and morals in terms of logical abstractions, but morality does have a locus—the cultural community. The essence of the moral life is the acceptance of restriction. For man there can be an infinite number of "thou shalt nots," and each culture decides on these behavioral codes.

If a child is educated within an ethnic group or cultural community, the moral injunctions he receives will not be abstract rules, but the concrete convictions and conventions of his group as expressed in their lives. To the child's question of "who am I?" the parent can reply, "you are X, therefore this is what you can or cannot do." Such an explanation, by way of one's communal identity, represents the most powerful inhibition of personal excess.

It is only when the impersonal state dissolves these cultural censors that man can be persuaded to commit the bestial acts that we have seen occur during history. For the general malaise of alienation, immorality and despair, the only solution is the human one, participation as an individual in a community where one can find a sense of identity, a belief in a shared set of values. An individual man cannot freely assent to or identify with values that are purportedly shared by hundreds of millions of people; hundreds yes, perhaps thousands. But with each step beyond, the bonds of humanity are stretched to the breaking point.

There is another right of culture that has been stifled in our modern era. This is life's innovative and creative dimension. Every generation has the right, indeed the necessity, to recreate the symbols, the ideals and meanings of its own society. In a culture in which the controls are so far removed from the average individual and in which men are recipients rather than recreators of the values and attitudes of their environment, it is not surprising that there is so much apathy and cynicism. Citizens, Aristotle once stated, must have the capacity to rule as well as be ruled in turn. The man who has some creative control over the work he does, the environment in which he lives, and the rules he has to follow, who participates in building his culture, is likely to be an enthusiastic, happy, and altruistic human being. If he learns that he is being manipulated for another's profit or exploited for the larger system, can we expect anything other than sullen hostility? Multiply this condition of each person millions of times and it is reasonable to expect conditions leading eventually to the dissolution of society.

The world does not have to be split into hundreds of thousands of cultures to fit this ideal of creative involvement for every individual. There are enormous possibilities within the great language cultures, each of which has an almost infinite number of possible gradations and subtleties beyond mere differences in dialect, customs, literature, or folklore. Each nation has well-recognized regional cultures which, given a modicum of independence and limitations on size, contain important possibilities for development and improvement. There has to be toleration for the uniqueness of each variant and exploration of its possibilities for cultural development and innovation. It must be protected so as not to degenerate into a satellite of London, Paris, or New York. This means that men will have to seek forms of internal development different from the usual improvement of roads, attracting factories to lower tax rates and the like. The need is for freedom of action and the wherewithall to be able to use this autonomy with sensitive leadership.

Johan Huizinga, in his important *Homo Ludens*, discusses the manner in which the entire fabric of culture seems to be permeated by conventional rules, suffused with ritual symbolism, pageantry, and formalism, in a diverse range of activity, from war to economics and sport.[13] The spirit of the "game" infects the activities of man in all cultures and in all historical epochs. Whether or not man can be described as *Homo ludens* or *Animal symbolicum*, the possibilities and permutations of

13 Johan Huizinga, *Homo Ludens* (Boston: Beacon Press, 1955).

conventional cultural behavior are practically infinite. The important fact about culture is that man needs to participate actively in this play. He should be a member of the team, wear its colors, have the opportunity either to play on the field, be alternately coach, cheerleader, or bandsman, depending on his abilities. It might be useful to explore the significance of the commonly held assertion that our own citizens are the most avid spectators since the days of the late Roman Empire.

Cultural Democracy

It takes relatively little to create a culture—time, spatial propinquity, naturally shared needs, activities, and interests, above all the freedom to pursue in a somewhat autonomous manner, the various dimensions of social life. Thus after the disintegration of Roman civilization, when general political disorder destroyed communication and transportation, small social enclaves all over Europe were gradually transformed into practically autonomous cultural unities, even under the successive Merovingian and Carolingian dynasties. In the eleventh and twelfth centuries, scarcely five hundred years after the collapse of the Roman West, there were literally dozens of Latin dialects, all representing incipient cultures, having their own historic traditions, local customs, crafts, songs, and a real sense of identity and unity. In the university towns of the twelfth and thirteenth century this diversity of peoples was epitomized in the various student nations given formal recognition by the authorities. At the University of Paris in the thirteenth century, France itself was represented by a number of different geographical and linguistic groups.

The Middle Ages was a time of religious oppression and feudalism. In addition, intellectually, it regressed from the classical eras. Yet, it was a period of great tolerance for cultural and political diversity. The age of the high Gothic, from A.D. 1100-1350 represents one of the richest eras of artistic creativity, intellectual curiosity, and even personal freedom. [14] It was a hierarchical period, true, but privilege had its limits and the several orders and classes had established roles in the society

[14] Friedrich Heer, *The Medieval World* (Cleveland: The World Publishing Co., 1962).

and enjoyed their own particular occupational panoply.[15] The existence of thousands of different political enclaves made passports and visas irrelevant and did not seem to inhibit travel. Students, artists, poets, and scholars wandered freely over the land. (There was none of the rigid division of age groups that exists in our own time. Young and old were mixed together, in all kinds of activities; function called forth the person, not age.)[16] Along with incipient nations, there were innumerable baronial fiefdoms, the free cities of Northern Italy, France, and the low countries, and the Hanseatic League.

The explosion of culture and intellect in the West begins at this time and continues in intermittent bursts until the beginning of the twentieth century. It was an outgrowth of the heterogeneous cultural freedoms tacitly recognized by these eras. It should be emphasized that the overt achievements of this era would not have been possible without the silent and relentless accumulation of cultural experience in the various and fragmented parcels of human habitation of the early medieval. We see only the overt manifestations of this silent process of germination. But psychic and cultural resources for the flowering of European culture were nevertheless being created in the manors and in the villages of countless communities of the Dark Ages. People were building a new set of historical experiences that would allow them to replace the disastrous Roman epoch with a new kind of Europe.

The consequent cultural freedoms are exemplified in the work of the peoples of Europe, diverse, unregulated, full of an impulse of creativity that was not isolated by virtue of its geographical or cultural separation from the parallel work of other peoples elsewhere. This earlier era had its share of the power hungry, of wars and oppression. Yet for the most part conflict was for political and economic status and the lives of the common folk were not affected. It was an era of material lack and cultural richness. The upper classes, having uncontested power and their own aristocratic cultural purview, attacked only their fellows, leaving the values of other classes uncompromised.

[15] Sylvia Thrupp, *The Merchant Class of Medieval London* (Ann Arbor: The University of Michigan Press, 1962).
[16] Philippe Ariés, *Centuries of Childhood* (New York: Random House, Inc., 1965).

When under the aegis of science and technology, modernism swept over Europe in the eighteenth and nineteenth centuries, cultural creativity in the humanities and arts enjoyed an even greater florescence—rather than being impeded, as might have been expected. The new intellectual movement had stimulated a variety of new esthetic forms in music, literature, architecture, and painting. Europe up to 1871 had not been encompassed by the philosophy of national and cultural hegemony. There were still many Germanies, each enjoying independence and bearing rich cultural fruit. The Austrian Empire was a conglomerate of minorities. It demanded and sometimes obtained political fealty rather than psychic submission.

As new national states began to appear in the 1830's, a search for and recognition of their largely hidden resources, now wedded to modern forms of artistic expression helped to apprise men of the powerful creative possibilities inherent in even the most submissive and undeveloped cultures. The spiritual advance of the Russian people from the time of Pushkin in the late eighteenth century to the great era of literature and music at the end of the nineteenth century is an example of the kinds of cultural energy and innovation that can coexist even with political and economic autocracy.

Cultural democracy thus is not the promulgation of a new right or a new liberty. It has been an implicit quality of social living throughout history. It exemplifies the natural unfolding of the creative nondiscursive symbols of thought. It is a right that has been fought for with great tenacity and viciousness. The religious wars of the past and present were focused on precisely this nondiscursive area of beliefs. Strip man of his wealth and he will not fight as hard as he would to protect the seemingly least important symbol of his religious identity. The Jews are a good example of the strength and power of self-conscious belief against various centralist attempts at conformity. The ghetto not only kept them isolated from the centers of power. It insulated them against the dissipation of their sense of uniqueness.

At the beginning of the modern era at Augsburg in 1555 and again at Westphalia in 1648, the rights of religious minorities were accounted for to be respected and guarded in their disestablishment from the contesting of political rivals. In the quickening pace of political and social change that followed, responsible leaders still heeded these ancient diversities that seemed to defy external manipulations of land and wealth. But in our own century a gradual change in the character of educated opinion concerning these rights can be discerned. As one commentator explains it:

> The collective rights of minorities was greatly enlarged by the Congress of Vienna in 1815, which not only guaranteed equality of civil and political rights to Christian confessions but, for the first time, the civil rights of Jews as a minority community. At the same time it guaranteed to the Polish minorities the right to representation in national institutions in Russia, Austria, and Prussia; and this meant the recognition of minority rights for the Polish population in those countries. It was a portentous precedent.[17]

Elizabeth Mann Borgese further notes that the Treaty of Berlin in 1879 extended these rights by establishing that transfer of territory to new political lands should in no way compromise the religious, civil, and political liberties of minorities groups. But with the League of Nations we note a hesitancy to encroach upon the sovereignty of states. In effect, the state was given almost carte-blanche rights to extend its powers, not only over the external actions of minority groups, but into the very existence of the minority culture. The power might be communicated in various forms of brutality and suppression in totalitarian nations, or subversion, coercion, and erosion in the "democratic" states. By its emphasis on the powerful economic and political dimensions and in its mechanistic individualism, the modern era has reflected its intellectual bias. In overlooking that man is more than a political and economic atom, we have forgotten the deepest and most fundamental bastion against the reductionism of state power—the cultural minorities.

The nature of equality thus has special relevance to cultural democracy. One kind of democracy strives for equality before the law, economic and social opportunities, and social and intellectual freedom. The opportunity for the utilization of these rights enhances a man's status *qua* man. But what of the democratic society where the egalitarian opportunities can be

17 Elizabeth Mann Borgese, "The Other Hill," *The Center Magazine* (July 1968), p. 5.

enjoyed only within a social structure of economic accumulation? What is the purpose of economic consumption even on a superbly exuberant level, in and of itself? What does it do to the individual and his community? It does provide some real physical conveniences. But in general it surrounds him only with a glittering array of toys and trinkets.

The economic dimension thus serves the shallowest ends of human individuality. Its all encompassing pursuit, so different from the shared consummations of the more ideational qualities of social life, divides man from man. Material possession, as Dewey once pointed out, inevitably separates, whereas the possession of a common art inevitably unites. Even more tragically, a democracy of economic pursuits and fulfillments constitutes the most puerile and barren of social endeavors. It is a total waste of the potentialities inherent in man's creative powers.

On the other hand, the use of these freedoms to liberate man for the "choice of continuous initiative," as Graham Wallis once stated, will ultimately result in a more substantive pluralism. The existence of communities of divergent interests and allegiances, where egalitarian opportunities have become realities, constitute buffers against the qualitative homogeneity that the centralists need as a precondition to their Holopolitan planning. [18]

Thus it is possible that functioning and semiautonomous minorities might indeed find more enriching uses of their share of the national wealth than new automobiles or color television sets. But then perhaps, as the philosophers said with some sadness when refusing to look through Galileo's telescope at Jupiter's moons, "the whole beautiful system might fall to the ground."

Pluralism and Power

Let us turn to a more practical view of the problem of pluralism to investigate the structure of the power inherent in and exercised by the state in the area of culture. A recent exemplification of the problem of universality and plurality is

---

[18] Clive Entwhistle, in the *New York Times* (August 10, 1968), describes a New York City of twenty million people, completely "planned" in every mechanical and human detail. A forthcoming study of his is to be called *Holopolis: Towards a Civilization.*

contained in the Civil Rights Bill of 1964.[19] This law has made less likely the use of race as a basis for the making of decisions affecting individuals. Henceforth, in a number of social areas, such as job opportunities, public accommodations, and voting, exclusion based upon race or ethnic background becomes a federal offense. Equality and universality are propositions applied through the power invested in the national government to prevent limitations in the freedom of citizens, regardless of race.

As a result, the supposed cultural freedoms of some have been invaded. What has heretofore been thought of as an area of private cultural behavior has been divested of its exclusivity and assigned to the larger public domain of law. Reason as exercised by our national government has thereby ruled that the cultural rights formerly exercised by a portion of our society (the South) have been illegitimately appropriated to deny other citizens of what is now deemed a universal privilege.

On the other hand, the bill has a specific exclusion. One area of economic enterprise, in manufacture and the employment of individuals, is exempted from the universality principle. The American Indian is now allowed to exclude all others from his traditionally private domain of endeavor—the production of arts, crafts, and other American Indian artifacts.

Implicit in this action is a recognition of the function that certain economic endeavors have for the maintenance of the cultural existence of groups. In addition, it is recognized that the Indian, through the effects of this discriminatory practice, will exert little pressure or power over his alien neighbors. Finally, the action deprives few non-Indians of their rights as American citizens. Thus Indian arts and crafts have been extracted from the universal symbolic arena and placed in the nondiscursive areas where pluralism and privacy thrive.

Were there other forms of economic enterprise closely related to the cultural existence of groups, other forms of exclusivity might be sanctioned. In cases of this sort, the criteria that must be tested in this balance between an equality that points toward uniformity and the cultural rights of communities in a pluralistic society, are justice and rationality. Are the special prerogatives granted to a group part of its genuine cultural as-

[19] *Civil Rights Act of 1964*, Public Law 88-352.

pirations, or are they masks behind which the group attempts to gain special privileges for itself to the detriment of others?

To underline this issue of the status of the symbols of power, we will reiterate an important argument in our discussion. Man's social existence is completely conditioned by his ideational involvements. The materiality of his existence is not what perturbs or excites him. It is rather the symbolic meaning that he gives to these material events:

> No longer in a merely physical universe, man lives in a symbolic universe. . . . No longer can man confront reality immediately; he cannot see it, as it were face to face. Physical reality seems to recede in proportion as man's symbolic activity advances. Instead of dealing with the things themselves man is in a sense constantly conversing with himself. He has so enveloped himself in linguistic forms, in artistic images, in mythical symbols or religious rites that he cannot see or know anything except by the interposition of this artificial medium. His situation is here the same in the theoretical as in the practical sphere. Even here man does not live in a world of hard facts, or according to his immediate needs and desires. He lives in the midst of imaginary emotions, in hopes and fears, in illusion and disillusions, in his fantasies and dreams. "What disturbs and alarms man" said Epictetus, "are not the things, but his opinions and fancies about things."[20]

The lack of equality in any society does not necessarily imply that some have material goods while others do not. This, of course, is a truism, but it has significant implications. Rather than look at the unequal distribution of goods among people, we should concentrate on a people's capacity to utilize, develop, and enjoy its full symbolic powers. It is conceivable that a materially wealthy society might be totally impoverished. In all eras some men have freely chosen to be poor. Certainly the Christian saints and the ascetics of all religions and cultures, even the bohemians, beatniks, and hippies of our own century, who renounce material indulgence, can be considered free as long as one necessary condition is met. Do they by their choice of life lose influence over their own and their society's destiny? Is there some inequality in which they partake by the mere choice of one set of values, in this case the renunciation of

[20] Ernst Cassirer, *An Essay on Man* (New Haven: Yale University Press, 1962), p. 25.

materialism? Does the man of wealth have more influence than others over the choices that are made in the political and social realm? If these conditions can be established, as is easily confirmed in our own culture, then we have the makings of an undemocratic society.

The philosophical position here being proposed argues that man's inner potentialities can often be more completely fulfilled by those in the lower social stratum than by those in power. The usurpation of power by any one group does not automatically bring with it all the rewards of social life. Rather these can be negated by the vision of life perpetuated by the ruling group. An extreme example of this is the slave society of the South in the nineteenth century. The white minority exercised complete power over the physical beings of the Negro. They enjoyed luxuriant surroundings that still fill us with awe. But what did they do with their power? How did they enhance themselves and the culture around them? As Vernon Parrington has described it, though they set forth for themselves the ideals of a Greek democracy, predicated upon a slave-holding society, their deeds were barren of fruit.[21] Education, culture, and intellectual ferment were soon nonexistent. Jefferson's great University in Charlottesville became a shadow of its former self. Little existed of depth or significance beside the social graces and embellishments with which the aristocracy surrounded itself.

On the other hand, the Negro, having little in the way of material resources, fell back on those hidden symbolic sources of meaning that were beyond the philosophical awareness and therefore control of the white ruling class. As a result of this, the Southern Negro has given us rich sources of musical inspiration, religious and moral depth and conviction, humor, and personality structure. Certainly, by comparison with his masters, the Negro probed the cultural possibilities of his environment more deeply than the white. And yet because of the power structure in which the Negro was enslaved and because of the philosophical bias we have towards the external accouterments of social life—the mansions, the clothes, the physical lassi-

---

[21] Vernon L. Parrington, *Main Currents in American Thought* (New York: Harcourt, Brace & World, 1954), Vol. II, pp. 94-130.

tude—we have a rather warped view of the relative values in this culture. The Negro himself looks upon all distinct manifestations of Negro culture with embarrassment as a bitter memory of a slave society. Yet America's most important and historic cultural achievement, jazz, is the product of the Negro. The tragic debasement of American slavery still allowed a fertile area of privacy within which these cultural seeds could germinate.

Many Jews likewise consider the cultural creations derived from the ghettos of Eastern Europe to be a painful reminder of less fortunate times. They find it difficult to perceive their beauty and emotional depth because of the social, economic, and political degradation in which the culture was fixed. The Yiddish memory has been replaced with the more prestigious Hebrew Biblical or Torah tradition. This traditional Yiddish culture now proceeds steadily toward extinction because of its rejection by the now affluent and accepted Jew. It is the victim of an aberrant and confused philosophy.

We have argued that it is necessary to regulate the role of government more closely with regard to the cultural values of society. Consistent and historic attempts have been made to deny social rights to cultural dissenter. The implication here is that the government should be neutral in regard to cultural values. Fortunately for mankind, autocracies usually demanded the subservience of society in the superficial materialistic paraphernalia of culture and left men's more significant cultural rights in peace. This has allowed for the free flow of creative ideas in spite of the superficial military, political, and even social changes at the top. The philosophical shallowness of these elites only facilitated the development by the subservient cultures of deeper strands of thought—philosophy, poetry, religion, and art.

Today those who practice the art of power manipulation have a more sophisticated grasp of the dynamics of human behavior, for there are now philosophical barriers to the open seizures of power. We now have as many kinds of "democracy" as kinds of government existed in the past. The existence and possibilities of the nondiscursive qualities of thought have been revealed by psychoanalysis and anthropology. The hidden manipulators of the minds and will of the masses have not been countered as yet. A wide range of human freedoms still lie unexplored and unrevealed. It is thus more necessary than ever to clarify the nature of the democratic society as predicated on the basis of heterogeneity rather than homogeneity.

Twentieth Century Cultural Pluralism Reevaluated

We can best elaborate on the contemporary challenges to American democracy by reexamining the problem of cultural pluralism as it relates to the symbolic philosophy here being offered. It has been argued that the pluralistic vision is basic to human nature and that it will manifest itself eventually in all societies, even those mass societies in which size has rendered diversification of behavior significant only in those most private interpersonal relations. Such was the general condition that existed in the United States in the 1920's. Yet the ethnic communities that were established at that time have by and large been dissipated and with them much of the vigor and diversity of our culture.

If the needs of man for cultural uniqueness are rooted in human nature, how were the pluralistic demands of the ethnic groups dissolved? Horace Kallen had expected that despite the great pressures of assimilation, the minorities would attempt to retain their natural rights. It is unnatural for man to surrender so easily that which is basic to his existence. Kallen, as we have noted, believed that ethnic values in America would go underground if they were not allowed to flourish freely.

That they did not go underground does not necessarily imply fallacious reasoning on Kallen's part. Nor is it necessarily supportive of I. B. Berkson's laissez-faire theory, which explicitly sanctions the dissolution of cultural minorities if they are not strong enough to survive the challenges of the larger society. Kallen correctly claimed that man's pluralistic needs run deep within his nature. They signify the existence of much deeper qualities of mind than the intellectual instrumentalism that Dewey conceived as the function of pluralism. Dewey's vision that shared intelligence contribute to the widening vistas of social experience, even into the international arena, was a laudatory aspiration. It neglected, however, the noninstrumental and the nonsurvivalistic concerns of thought that exist in this deeper stratum of the human personality. Scientific intelligence exists both to pursue for its own sake the cognitive elements in man's symbol-making proclivities as well as to secure the free expression of the mythic and nondiscursive qualities of human perception.

We have noted previously a possible reason for the dissipation of traditional ethnic pluralism in the 1930's and 1940's— external political and social causes. But there were also deeper reasons. Man finds it difficult to translate his inchoate perception of freedom into actuality without the guidance of a philosophy that explains to him his needs and rights. During the 1930's and 1940's there was little guidance or support of this sort. Because of this, ethnic affiliations were subject to considerable attrition by the current philosophies of assimilation, especially as the philosophies were couched in humanitarian and democratic terms.

With the Great Depression and later World War II came sharper challenges to man's symbolic existence, at times brute physical survival. All of our available psychic energies were spent in returning the larger system to stability, temporarily submerging our concern for ethnic culture. The existing power structure still explicitly propounding traditional Anglo-Saxon culture, especially through the public school, disseminated through the communication media a set of meanings instrumental for and yet far transcending the practical needs of the time. The mythic qualities of the New Deal and the charismatic force of Franklin D. Roosevelt were elements that helped fuse together the diverse cultures into a unity that was carried into World War II. The fullest participation of all sectors of our heterogeneous society was necessary to ensure victory.

As stated above, the weight assembled by the entire society to gain unity of social intent far exceeded the necessary goals of military, political, or economic unity. But the people were not philosophically aware of their cultural rights. They were persuaded that economic, social, and political unity demanded the sacrifice of their differences as a contribution to a democratic America. We can thus see that Berkson's laissez-faire pluralism, by which each ethnic group's devotion to its values is tested by its resistance to the pressures of the majority culture, is an unrealistic test of the validity of cultural pluralism. It places the greatest onus on those communities most vulnerable, the cul-

turally advanced and socially involved groups, and tacitly sanctions the pluralism that lives on only in the agricultural back-
water still untouched by an expansive mass culture. That
vigorous local cultures still existed at the close of the World
War II, now more fully participating in the American adventure,
yet still retaining an appreciation and cultivation of their special
values, further testifies to the stubbornness of man.[22]

CONCLUSION

The shift toward a more diversified allocation of power
which is suggested here carries with it an important qualification. It has never been possible for any community except for
the smallest and most isolated to be purely homogeneous in
make-up. For minorities exist within the minorities. History has
shown that the minorities have no better record of tolerance
than those at the centers of power. Therefore restraints must
exist on the actions of all groups.

For this we shall once more turn to the universal principle.
The persecutions, legal lychings, and witch hunts characteristic
of all groups given their sway cannot be tolerated under any
guise—local control, states rights, or even cultural pluralism. A
civilized world must demand the maintenance of certain universal human rights. No community should be free of the super-
visory scrutiny of the larger community of men. Due process is
a right of the dissenter, the "oddball," the black sheep, in every
social context, even the international.

We do argue for the right of diverse communities to maintain their own patterns and rules of life. This can involve clothing regulations, noise-level tolerance, Sunday blue laws, or vege-
tarianism. A community which has nothing unique about its
choice of values, has no consciousness of what it means to be a
constituent member, is not a community—it is an assemblage.
The tragedy of our time is that so many communities are no
more than a factory, a shopping center, and a place to sleep.

The right to disagree with the existing values of a community ought to be upheld, whether it is disagreement over general

[22] Ethel Albert, "Conflict and Change in American Values—A
Cultural-Historical Approach," *Ethics* (October 1963), pp. 19-33.

attitudes, with neighbors, or with town fathers. Anyone ought to be able to speak freely before a group of his peers to attempt to persuade them to his views. And if he fails, he ought to be able to remove himself to a more favorable environment.

The progress of the average community will be conditioned by a pragmatic test. If it outrages or exacerbates the young in its reluctance to adapt to change, the young will be sure to leave it and to consign it as a consequence to stagnation. Here the laissez-faire test ought to be applied. For there is a multitude of healthy towns and villages, even geographic areas, which could have provided its members with an alternative to the values of urban sprawl. The desertion of its constituents was not voluntary. It was forced by the state, which dispensed its economic largess in such a manner as to benefit certain areas and communities while it destroyed others, having equally viable social structures and as intensely loyal citizens.

chapter 5

Contemporary Social and Educational Issues

THE PLURALISTIC PHILOSOPHY

The test of any philosophical perspective lies in its power to illuminate the common-sense experiences of man and to clarify the contemporary problems that confront and afflict mankind. It must meet a real pragmatic test. Does the philosophy of cultural pluralism, in its reinterpretation through the symbolic point of view, help us to effect some practical changes in the existing situation? Does this philosophy at least give us a new way at looking at things that might lead eventually to choices different than those we might make today? To be meaningful, the philosophy should allow us to make pertinent decisions with regard to real issues, real institutions, real people.

As preparation for a discussion of some of the contemporary issues that can be clarified through the pluralistic position, it might be helpful to restate some of the essential assertions of this philosophy. These are derived both explicitly (from Ernst Cassirer's theory of knowledge, human nature, and culture) and implicitly (from extending the logic of Cassirer's thought into realms not explicitly discussed in his writings).

Recapitulation

There is an inner structure to cultural life that is composed of those diverse symbolic meanings essential for carrying out social intercourse. The natural tendency inherent in these subtle, nondiscursive, and personal forms of symbolic communication is a divergent rather than a convergent one. It gives rise to many different cultures distinctly pluralistic in the meaning and structure of their symbolism. The quality of life that gives specificity to each culture can be easily identified in this non-discursive symbolic realm: language, ritual, myth, play, sport, religion, personality and character structure, architecture, fine and applied arts, crafts, style, cuisine, music, sculpture, dance, drama, and literature. The contrasting tendency in discursive knowledge is toward more universal symbolic principles.

Social knowledge has come increasingly under the regulation of the universality principle as man has sought to establish more inclusive forms of equality. But the function of the equality principle is not to flatten the differences between men nor to search for absolute uniformity. Rather it is to ameliorate the inequalities of power that tend to inhibit man's essential nature. In a democratic society, where power is distributed equally to all groups and individuals, pluralism is the natural condition of cultural life. We hypothesize that societies large in both population and geography which have maintained cultural homogeneity have somehow inhibited the natural individuation of local communities.

Pluralism need not be imposed upon man or society. All that is needed for its natural realization is a social structure that allows real personal and community freedom. Perhaps an intellectual enunciation of the philosophical and practical dimensions of the concept is needed to suggest its utility. This enunciation might help to reveal to men what they themselves feel so deeply about.

The argument which follows is not to be considered as inclusive, but rather as synoptic and suggestive. The issues, both theoretical and practical, are vast; they outdistance the range of one author or one book. However, with the strong pressures exerted to effect amalgamation and centralism, the need for continuing discussion and debate is essential. The following pages are to be thought of as a small contribution to a necessary dialogue.

THE EDUCATION OF MINORITIES

The Context

Over fifty years ago American society confronted the apex of immigration and the variegated problems associated with the assimilation of the different ethnic minorities. Our society today is by and large homogeneous. Yet there are still minorities among us. They are not aliens from foreign lands pleading for admission into a country whose social traditions are already formed and established, but Americans, whose roots in our nation in some cases antedate the first Anglo-Saxon. They are the Negro, Puerto Rican, and Mexican, and their status in a complacent, wealthy society is approaching a state of crisis.[1]

They are the poor in search of jobs in a land where jobs are getting scarcer even for the majority. They inhabit the rotting central areas of cities whose heyday has long since passed and which the older minorities have deserted. Finally, and perhaps most important, the ethnic status of these minorities is conditioned and haunted by the spectre of racial apartheid.

The racial barrier against the minorities does not work equally against the three groups. Both Puerto Ricans and Mexicans find the barriers variable. The Mexicans, especially, maintain unique relationships with the Anglo-Saxon in the former's areas of heaviest concentration. A tenacious and prideful exaltation of their linguistic and cultural identities has given each—the Mexican and Puerto Rican—a distinct position in current discussions of segregation and exploitation of our minority groups.

In areas where, for example, Mexican Americans comprise a large minority or even a majority of the population, the defense of their cultural autonomy and integrity is so open as to defeat attempts by state-supervised public schools to impose the language, culture, values, and even the discursive knowledge of the larger society. Here the atmosphere is Spanish and even local "Anglos" voluntarily allow themselves to be absorbed, to a limited extent, in the Spanish view of things. This is not due to historical priority alone, as we can see if we contrast the relations of the Anglos to the Indian minorities. In the case of the Mexicans, an environment evolved that gave the pluralistic demands of the minority some possibility of realization. The philosophy of the great Puerto Rican leader, Muñoz Marin, that argues for a form of cultural parallelism which would be protected by the commonwealth status of Puerto Rico, is a discursive and rational manifestation of this desire. It is noteworthy

---

[1] Michael Harrington, *The Other America* (New York: Macmillan Company, 1962).

that, in the midst of the integrationist agitation of 1963-64, the Puerto Rican communities were content to set forth demands for jobs and housing as a community, having no intention to agitate for assimilation into the majority society.

The Negro and Integration

The status of the black man presents us with the most perplexing and difficult problems we have ever had to solve in relation to the traditional role of minorities. The twenty-one million black Americans have an historic involvement in our callous treatment of minorities. And their enslavement, liberation, and ensuing isolation in a cocoon of segregation sit heavily on the national conscience.

The position generally taken by the liberal community with regard to the black minority represents a significant reinterpretation of this problem. Since the 1954 Brown case, the views of this community on the three crucial concepts—segregation, desegregation, and integration—have conditioned all recent intellectualizations of the nature of social equality. It is important to counter these concepts, not only because they are in implicit opposition to the views presented in this study, but also because they would bring about the interment of values we propose to establish.

Desegregation as a concept implies that the use of force by the state against free choice in public services would be unlawful. The concept of integration came into our vocabulary largely because desegregation proceeded so slowly in the South. Also, the connotations of desegregation were primarily passive and thus lacked any positive philosophical or social values. The de facto separation of black people in the ghettos of Northern cities, along with notable deficiencies in educational achievement, employment, and opportunities for social advancement, made it necessary to enlarge the perspective produced by the Brown decision. Advocates of racial integration demanded a more prophetic social vision for the democratic ideal than the laissez-faire atmosphere of "with all deliberate speed" generated by the desegregation decision.

Integrationists today stress the equality and brotherhood of man, the necessity for disregarding social and cultural differences, and the need for unity, arguments similar to those advanced in the older assimilationist tradition. In addition, much stress is placed on the historic denial of Negro rights: "separate" has always meant unequal. Wherever de facto forms of segregation exist, Negro schools are poor, the houses slums, the streets filthy. There are few jobs for blacks; there is much intellectual and emotional impoverishment. Equality of opportunity under these circumstances, so the argument goes, is a tragic farce; the Negro remains inevitably at the bottom of the social ladder. Anything but an active program of integration of whites and blacks in schools, housing, and social practices will conspire to create further conditions of Negro inferiority.

According to this argument, the full integration of the black man into white society will not only break the pattern of Negro debasement but it will ameliorate the guilt that has been the white man's own special burden for so many hundreds of years. The mixing of children of all races and backgrounds in our schools will benefit both the Negro and the white child. For the Negro child it will provide an environmental challenge and stimulus for learning and advancement; for the white child it will constitute a real, rather than a verbal act of tolerance and brotherhood, an appreciation and respect for the fact that people of all backgrounds deserve equality. Integration will teach the white man a lesson in democracy that he cannot learn in a totally white culture. It will bring back to the white power structure a legitimacy that the external, legalistic act of desegregation could never achieve.

A deeper philosophical strand lies below the surface of the surge of assimilationist sentiment in favor of integration. This is an almost mystical belief of the majority of our people in an America that is greater than the sum of its social parts. Perhaps it is a remnant of an older Hegelian organicism, which conceives of a higher spiritual unity within which the political, social, and economic values of a nation are absorbed. The America of this ideology has one social façade into which all superficial differences are blended. It is an American version of Rousseau's *volonté général*, an ethos that obliterates differences and allows us to speak as a culture with but one voice.[2] The Negro, too, should and will be incorporated into this monolithic unity that is the true American tradition.

[2] On this concept in Rousseau see Edward Hallett Carr, *The New Society* (Boston: Beacon Press, 1957), p. 61.

Is Integration Possible?

This vision is antithetical to the proposals we have promulgated as being natural to human beings. What is being proposed by the integrationists is that the one largely undigested group in our society be freed to partake of the very malaise that affects us all. There is little thought, either by black leadership or by white supporters as to what exchange of values will take place.[3] We would be asking black people to exchange one form of inequality for another less personal perhaps, and therefore less fearsome.

Neither the truths explicated in the Brown decision nor in the Civil Rights Bill of 1964 can be rationally denied. Desegregation and nondiscrimination on the public level have great rational validity. Integration is a more subtle problem. It leaves the public area of the protection of rights to enter the private area of human association. It cannot force changes in private action except through undemocratic uses of power. Successful integration necessitates dual acquiescence. Both whites and blacks need to agree on a number of values to be shared henceforth uniformly and reciprocally.

Let us consider first the problem of white acquiescence. In Europe relations between cultural groups have been characterized by an inhering quality of reciprocity. Thus Germans and Poles, Italians and Englishmen have come together both in war and in peace. Even under the veneer of surface prejudice, the equality of all peoples has been tacitly acknowledged in spite of cultural differences. On the American continent, this accommodation of ethnic minorities has taken place fairly easily. But this element of reciprocity of cultural relations is so markedly absent between black and white as to inhibit effective social intercourse. The measure of possible integration can be found in the mutual acceptance by both groups of intermarriage.

But this is a cultural rather than a racial problem.[4] Witness

[3] See New York City Board of Education, *The Puerto Rican Study, 1953-1957* (New York, 1958).

[4] Dwight J. Ingle, "Racial Differences and the Future," *Science* (October 16, 1964), pp. 375-379, raises some pertinent questions over this issue and states that we need research that does not prejudge the results. See also, Arthur R. Jensen, "How Much Can We Boost IQ and Scholastic Achievement?" *Harvard Educational Review* (Winter 1969). Jensen argues that IQ depends much more on genetic than on environmental factors. His impressive document necessitates that we refrain from foreclosing the issue.

the comparative ease with which Oriental and white marriages are accepted in our society. If we study our treatment of black-white miscegenation, we find a good test of the black man's possible acceptance into those subtle and deeply personal social relations that groups share and out of which comes the union of diverse communities through marriage. The relationship of black and white has been unilateral. There has been a continuous introduction of white genes into the black American population, a situation that has deeply corrupted relations between the races. The black man has no claims of historic cultural parity, as do Chinese or Japanese, but merely the memory of being alternately debased and feared by the white. The white man will not accept integration, because he does not yet see the Negro as an equal; he cannot accept it because in his entire experience with black men, he has been the exploiter. Likewise, the black community, imprisoned in a white world in which it has always been the victim, is sterilized emotionally and intellectually by its sense of inferiority.[5]

Cultural Guilt

To the guilt- and fear-ridden white, the debasement of the black man has been complete and the average Negro is aware of this, even if not discursively.[6] As noted above, what black people have salvaged from their previous experience with the white majority culture are values that have escaped the scrutiny of the white man. Their religious vigor and involvement, their spirituals, humor, jazz, and even the warmth and intimacy of their personality are now admired by the white man from the outside.

Many Negroes see these characteristics as representing a slave culture. To the educated black person, imbued with discursive values derived from the white society, these "Uncle Tom" traits are to be avoided and abandoned at the first opportunity. But to the average Negro, these symbols are indeed

[5] It has taken a sensitive Negro from the French island of Martinique to express this issue both in personal as well as philosophical terms. See Frantz Fanon, *Black Skin, White Masks* (New York: Grove Press, Inc., 1967).
[6] See the judicious discussion of Charles E. Silberman in *Crisis in Black and White* (New York: Random House, Inc., 1964), pp. 109-122.

realities of life. They constitute his personality. Their aban-
donment represents his obliteration as a cultural being. Logically, of course, there is no defense for lumping together their
origins in slavery with their derivative social status in the cultural spectrum of our world, for these cultural characteristics
are achievements that in many ways transcend what the non-
slave society contributed to our culture.

From the standpoint of the symbolic philosophy, the dilemma of the Negro can be discussed in the following manner:
The cultural values that are shared by the group constitute the
materials from which self identity is made. If there is to be any
integrity of self, it must come from the respect, cultivation, and
practice of one's own world of symbolic meanings. Also, the
inherent equality of all values is a truth that is transmitted to
man below the surface of discursive thought. In fact, as a truth,
it transcends anything that one can say discursively to the contrary. Only in the face of the most subtle underminings and
exchanges of values can the tenacious hold of a people on its
culture be displaced. What can the black man accept in exchange for his identity, as rudimentary, underdeveloped, and
one-sided as it may be?

In truth, black people may not want to be integrated into
the majority society. As distant as they are from equality, as
compared with other minorities, this position adds to their re-
calcitrance to become the next addition to the larger society.
Black people are aware of the powerful but latent hostility that
will meet them if they step into the role the white liberal has
designed for them. As it is, today, as in any discourse between
minority and majority groups, the average Negro speaks two
languages, one directed to the white world, another addressed
to his fellows. How is this to be broken down under the conditions that exist?

If we hypothesize that blacks reject the integrationist thesis,
that they respect their cultural identity and refuse to sacrifice it
for the chimerical hope of union with the white majority, there
is reason to ask why there has been such wide acceptance of the
integration movement by educated black Americans. The answer lies in the tremendous power of philosophy in overcoming
the nonlogical truths of feeling, even if the philosophy is a
shallow, possibly even a mistaken, one. Today there is only one

respectable intellectual road toward equality and that is the current philosophy of integration.

Democracy has too often been linked to values of assimilation and cultural orthodoxy. It is because the universal lawlike status of scientific statements has been illegitimately imposed upon the realm of cultural values. Pluralism has thus gained only a shadowy and undefined philosophical substance. The black intelligentsia have been dependent upon white support for so long that they have largely accepted the latter's sociological viewpoint of knowledge. They have learned to share the white man's embarrassment over the black man's cultural roots. In this way, they find it easier to repress the visceral truths that are still largely unexpressed in discursive terms.

By contrast, the black masses in the slums are not enticed by the intellectualizations of the elite. They live by what nondiscursive values they have salvaged and that unfortunately now vegetate and deteriorate in the city slums. There is little opportunity for the black populace to develop whatever traditional areas of culture are left to them. The white society restricts both physically and mentally, enveloping through mass communications techniques all that remains of the mind space of creativity in Negro folk culture.

A peculiar situation has arisen because of the lack of communication between the black leadership and the *Lumpenproletariat* in the slums. Agitation for compulsory integration in the schools has largely been rejected by the masses. Their disinterest in the educational opportunities provided in open-enrollment schools is evidence of their evaluation of this philosophy as not only impossible of attainment but also unworthy of their aspirations. Further, they have manifested actions that still puzzle the white majority as well as the black leadership. The primitive social behavior of the black masses, the educational and political apathy, the moral degradation, crime, riots, and raw hate hardly manifest readiness for the integrationist struggles that lie ahead. Rather, they reflect a state of disinterest and of intellectual anarchy, possibly because none of the proposed philosophies strike a sympathetic chord in the mind of the average black person.

Black leadership, therefore, is not likely to realize its goals in the pursuit of such educational solutions, e.g., bussing, statistical population criteria of equality, racial percentages, artificial redistricting, and the like. One wonders how black leadership could have been persuaded to make such predications, for to do so was to place emphasis on the externals of what is a problem of substance. The white liberal's compliance in this respect seems understandable since it complements his own vision of an excellence by which the Negro ought to live.

More than likely, the frustrations will continue to grow and with them we will see a visible increase in interracial suspicions and hostility. We will see the fragmentation of black leadership and perhaps even its dissolution. That these may be our future options raises the possibility that the available avenues leading toward equality will be further narrowed.

Black Nationalists

A more explicit rejection of integration is found in the Black Muslim movement, in the activities of Malcolm X, slain leader of a parallel nationalistic group, and the various disciples of Malcolm now advocating "black power." Where the integrationist fights for the opportunity to be mixed with whites in all areas of life, especially education, for the uplifting and stimulating effect of association with white students and teachers, the nationalist groups reject any association with whites because of the demeaning and corrupting values that may be imputed to the black man by this association. Where the integrationist wants active governmental pressure for the mixing of the races so that, implicitly, the Negro might lose his identity and gain the values of the white society, the Muslim wants a separate state so that the integrity of the black race may be retained. Where integrationists maintain that dignity and morality lie with integration, the others state that their hope exists in separation.

The Muslims have not only argued in this manner; they have attempted to illustrate the truth of their claims. The orthodox of the sect are peaceful, moral, energetic, and hard-working.[7] They take pride in their race, religion, and culture. But in their perceptive exploitation of the hidden inner needs of their peo-

[7] C. Eric Lincoln, *The Black Muslims in America* (Boston: Beacon Press, 1961), pp. 80-83.

ple, they have gone further than necessary in their discursive analysis. They appeal to an obscure cultural allegiance and not to the rational, historical, and political truths that could garner for the movement a larger Negro following. Two Muslim claims actually clash with the realities and objectives of the Negro minority tradition: their religious focus and their demands for a separate nation. Protestant Christianity is too deeply rooted in Negro history and culture. Also, the black man has firm roots in the larger political and social mainstream of American history. The Muslims cannot prosper in the long run if they continue to refute their historic allegiances.

But the nationalist movement has broader support within the Negro community than in the past. Since the murder of Malcolm X the theme of black power has burst upon the American scene with a sudden, and to some, terrifying impact.[8] For it has coincided with the appalling riots and murders within the Negro ghettos of dozens of our cities. It is perhaps not too extreme to speak of these events as part of a new kind of revolution, albeit one that partakes of a hiatus during the winter months.

Recent black leaders, such as H. Rap Brown, Stokely Carmichael, and Eldridge Cleaver, represent the vanguard of a militancy that derives its support from the masses in the slums. Rage, rhetoric, and hatred are the real expression of the repressed feelings of these people. The riots, burning, and looting are also representative, but they are a physical and non-verbal manifestation of these repressed feelings. Yet the political or intellectual leadership does not exist that is prepared to meet and negotiate these grievances with a majoritarian white superstructure.

What we have seen since 1965 adequately expresses the feelings of the Negro poor, who for so long had been unrepresented, except by the few Negro intellectuals and leaders who cultivated the elitism of W. E. B. Dubois, without his radical politics. This traditional leadership has gradually awakened to the state of affairs. We have seen the defections of Whitney Young of the Urban League to the philosophy of black power

[8] Stokely Carmichael and Charles Hamilton, *Black Power* (New York: Random House, Inc., 1968).

and the commitment of the Reverend Milton Galamison, formerly a leader in the integrationist movement, to the cause of decentralization and community (black) control of local urban school districts. This ideological turnabout was consequently honored in Rev. Galamison's nomination to the Board of Education of New York City, to aid in the process of decentralization.

We do not claim that the black nationalist movement exemplifies a wide acceptance of the philosophy of pluralism. But the Negro's insistence that his negritude be valued and that white coercions and paternalism be rejected has its roots in the pluralist interpretation of human nature and its illumination of the sources of human dignity. The future of the pluralistic vision of the black man is dependent upon a number of variables. At present it is only a reaction of frustration and rage against the dominant society. There are two competing dynamics in this situation. One is the attempt by our government under the aegis of white and black liberal integrationist views to bring the black masses into the middle class—through various welfare, job, and housing programs, and through educational upgrading. This represents the traditional assimilationist patterns that succeeded in another era and for other cultural groups. Both through tangible expenditures of money and through the legal elimination of constraint in every area of social life it is hoped that the race problem will be solved as the black population is dispersed into the white middle class.

It has been a feeble effort, due partly to conservative legislators and partly to an economically debilitating war. We have hardly touched conditions in the ghetto except to exacerbate Negro impatience. Because progesss is so slow, the Negro mood is bordering on complete violence and anarchy. White receptiveness has hardened, the flight from the city accelerated, and the general incarceration of the majority of the Negroes made even more complete.

At this point the second dynamic pattern emerges. Knowing that their right to equality is violated and not having institutional patterns of amelioration, black power has become the only currently meaningful expression of the Negro condition. Black political control, the "takeover" of black schools, the creation of black arts festivals, indeed the general enunciation that "black is beautiful," reflect a natural but perhaps temporary set of symbols appealing to the Negro, in the absence of the economic emoluments promised by the white society.

But let us ask ourselves how the black nationalist movement would fare philosophically were the massive rehabilitations promised by the white power structure to be realized? The endemic disorganization of Negro cultural life makes us doubtful that if given the material appurtenances of the middle class there would be much immediate interest in the development of a black culture. Thus, in spite of all that we have heard of black separatism, we might see black power vanish through a minimal amelioration of the material plight of the Negro.

This is not to say that the Negro dreams of integration. Neither does the white majority. By bettering the life of the urban Negro, improving his schools, providing the possibilities for the creation of an indigenous elite and even a homegrown intelligentsia a massive flight of Negroes to the suburbs might be stemmed. Both black and white realize that geographical propinquity to the white man is not in itself either necessary or sufficient for attaining the social and material advantages of the middle class.

One would like to suppose that the conditions are present for a pluralistic cultural vision in the black community's desire for self-determination, both politically and educationally. Yet on historic evidence it is improbable that a people could make the transition from poverty to egalitarian pluralism without first obtaining the various material benefits of our technology (and with them the bland identity of the culture of technology). It is saddening that the current black power mood denies to the Negro masses even the minimal dignity engendered by these economic advantages.

The development of an educated, indigenous black leadership aware of the necessity for slow construction within the framework of the larger national culture, developing standards of achievement consonant with full participation, yet reserving an important dimension of energy for the creation of a rich Negro cultural life is not on the immediate horizon. Yet it is, as the director and actress Barbara Ann Teer has expressed, ultimately crucial for the survival of the Negro:

Our salvation is in developing our own black theater forms supported by strong cultural philosophies.

Culture is simply the total way of life built up by a group of human beings and transmitted from one generation to another. That definition is very important because the theater is one way of transmitting cultural forms. That means that the way we walk, the way we sing, dance, pray, laugh, eat, curse, "hit on a girl," make love and, most important, the way we look, make up our cultural heritage. Our culture is rich and beautiful; there is nothing like, or equal to, the black life style. It is uniquely and intimately our personal gift to the world. . . .

We must begin building cultural centers where we can enjoy being free, open and black, where we can find out how talented we really are, where we can be what we were born to be, and not what we were brainwashed to be, when we can literally "blow our minds" with blackness. The white establishment does not have the time, knowledge, inclination or intelligence to do our research for us and furthermore it is not their responsibility, it is ours. Besides, the "man" has reached a dead end creatively so why should we continue to take our problems to him? He can't even solve his own problems, let alone ours.

So let's forget him, brothers and sisters; turn your minds and your feet around; head for home.[9]

Minority Jew and Negro

A comparison of the Jew with the Negro evokes some interesting cultural contrasts. The Jew did not deny his identity when faced with degradation and persecution. Rather, he emphasized his cultural uniqueness. The prejudices and pressures of the majority became a constant goad to purify and improve the culture; they did not breed apathy or hopelessness. A result of this attitude was the historic Jewish ego, which not only produced the pride and self-respect necessary for learning, but which usually encouraged activity at higher peaks than the outside world. Thus to anti-Semitic imprecations, the Jew replied with a silent affirmation of his own superiority.

Today, after surrendering the bulk of his cultural inheritance for a measure of social, political, and economic freedom, there are urban and suburban Jews who still prefer to live in what to all intents and purposes are segregated Jewish areas.

[9]*New York Times*, July 7, 1968. Copyright © 1968 by the New York Times Company. Reprinted by permission.

These areas are not slums, nor are the inhabitants demanding egress into Gentile areas, either in housing or schooling.[10] The Jew seems to be satisfied with himself because he has made a minimum of concessions to the majority culture. But he now strives to defend the little cultural autonomy he has retained. There is, in fact, an active attempt by the Jewish community to avoid any further integration into the larger society.[11]

The Jews have contributed to the larger society in a variety of forms, largely because of the symbolic resources available to them as Jews. Had they been forced to defend their minority status on the basis of their supposed cultural inferiority, as the Negro has done, we would see a different result.

A Reinterpretation

Before the Negro can make demands upon the larger society for the freedoms that are properly his, he needs a perspective of his condition that is intellectually supportable. As long as members of the majority white community see the Negro as a member of a unique community while the integrationist leaders act as if there is none and so long as the black power advocates see their goal solely as revenge, no progress can be expected. The shame the black man feels for himself, manifested in all of these philosophical extremes, is the most tragic of the many undemocratic imputations of inferiority that the majority American culture has made.

In both anthropological and historical literature there is ample evidence of the inherent importance and value of every underdeveloped culture. Reason and discursive thought are not given to man *de novo*. They are gradually constructed from the nondiscursive mythic and esthetic symbols of all rich folk cultures. It is thus necessary for every developing community to have a self-conscious awareness of its symbolic values.

[10] See Herbert Gans, *The Urban Villagers*. This book relates how a well-structured low income Italian community in Boston maintained a rich neighborhood culture in surroundings that might have become slums until a misguided urban-renewal program destroyed their tenements as well as their community.

[11] This concern with "integration" is reflected in Dr. Erich Rosenthal's report on mixed marriages in the *1963 American Jewish Year Book*, American Jewish Committee (New York: The Free Press, 1963). It shows a rate of intermarriage of 17.9 percent in Washington, D.C.

We ought not as a matter of democratic justice ask black Americans to reject a culture that has existed for three hundred years. True, this culture has been deprived and debased; we only now see the extent to which this has been accomplished. We need to find a way of overcoming the extremes of nationalistic self-annihilation in violence and hatred and the integrationist attempt to achieve the same end through assimilation and hopeless miscegenation.

Through a period of several generations, the two vital dimensions of rational intelligence could be developed—the universal qualities of the discursive scientific and the warmer personal nuances of the nondiscursive, his own culture. It could be done through education. Our lack of a conscious philosophical attempt to deal with the problem of the black man's unique minority status—his race in a Protestant Anglo-Saxon culture— has already resulted in disaster for countless valuable human beings. [12]

In forcing him to compete with white children far better prepared for their kind of education than he is, the Negro has encountered defeat and frustration without understanding the cultural sources for his difficulties. [13] His educational failure is real enough, but it is caused by deeper factors than the de facto segregated housing or schooling of our Northern cities. The problems do not lie in his external circumstances, especially when the overt power of public institutions has been removed, as directed by the Brown decision of 1954. Nor is it being apart from his white brothers that allegedly makes the black man inferior. [14]

The cause is similar to the cultural and intellectual status of all enslaved and dominated peoples of the past. The cause of Negro educational laxity lies predominantly in the inferiority

[12] See Stanley M. Elkins, *Slavery* (New York: Grosset & Dunlap, Inc., 1963), which describes the uniquely debasing character of Anglo-Saxon Protestant forms of slavery.

[13] See Charles E. Silberman, *Crisis in Black and White* (New York: Random House, Inc., 1964), pp. 298-299.

[14] Kenneth Clark and Lawrence Plotkin show that students from Southern segregated high schools did better as scholarship students in Northern colleges than their confrères from the Northeastern, supposedly nonsegregated environments. "The Negro Student at Integrated Colleges" in A. Harry Passow et al. (eds.), *Education of the Disadvantaged* (New York: Holt, Rinehart & Winston, Inc., 1968).

felt by each Negro from the first time he realizes his difference from the white majority.[15] Most often, this feeling of inferiority arises from the earliest direct confrontation of white and black. Subsequent interracial contacts so quickly and deeply embed the connotation of social and cultural inferiority that growth in the intellectual spheres is conclusively undermined.[16]

This minority has had to face a nihilistic detraction both because of the obviousness of its racial differences and because its group alone has been emasculated of all cultural pride. The very qualities of uniqueness and reinvigoration that minority cultures have been able to contribute to the health and welfare of the larger society have been the target of both white and Negro leadership. Thus the hoped-for basis of intellectual growth has been effectively inhibited. The child, bereft of community or family support, draws upon more primitive psychological supports to ensure his existence as a person. The visible manifestations of this quality of the mind—the defense mechanisms, the sullen hostility to education, the emotive ferocity of slum life, the pervasive cultural paranoia—are an attempt to counter this process of psychic annihilation.[17] Is it any wonder that there is so little emotional or intellectual freedom within the average Negro child to play with ideas, to develop that disinterested intellectual curiosity that is the prolegomenon to the process of advanced educational achievement?

It is the black man himself who must say what is necessary for his educational development. It is not likely that he would plan the educational parks (prisons?) such as those proposed for Chicago, that will immerse both white and black in vast complexes apart from their own communities; these are the grisly, cacophonic creations of bureaucratic system builders. Black people are more likely to plan for neighborhood schools, whether they be white, black, or mixed.

---

[15] A. R. Guilliland, in *Child Development*, cited by Dwight J. Ingle, "Racial Differences and the Future," *Science* (October 16, 1964), pp. 375-379.

[16] Kenneth B. Clark and M. P. Clark, "The Emergence of Racial Identification and Preference in Negro Children," in *Readings in Social Psychology*, E. Maccoby et al., (eds.), 3rd ed. (New York: Holt, Rinehart & Winston, Inc., 1958).

[17] William Grier and Price M. Cobb, *Black Rage* (New York: Basic Books, Inc., 1968).

Such decentralized school districts could be the structural beginning for the growth of a diversified community life, cultural, social, and political. Each community needs its own set of institutions, some purely local and some representative of the wider state and national political entities. Whether they be post offices, state or federal office buildings, even agencies of international bodies, they should mingle with purely local creations. The neighborhood schools, churches, community centers, the theaters, stores, skilled artisans, business and corporate offices all contribute to the total life perceptions of its people. To isolate the children, whether they are six or sixteen years of age, to transport them miles away to be inundated with thousands of other children, apart from all contextual educational experiences, is to accept irrationality as a guide for educational planning.

Irving Kristol, noting the manner in which extremists have taken over recently to enact local "model cities" projects of the federal government, has wondered at the efficacy of decentralization in the context of our times.[18] Further, he has noted, with Daniel P. Moynihan's concurrence, that the Negro middle class has attained its place in the recent past through great city, state, and national bureaucracies. Were decentralization, local control, and pluralism to become the predominant forces in our nation, would not the Negro be segregated once more from the larger society? Kristol's first concern can be countered rather simply. Democratic processes of self-management always involve dangers. But this is no reason to try more autocratic forms. Given fuller participation by communities, the demagogues as well as the sycophants would no doubt be quieted. As was pointed out earlier, no community should be given carte blanche to exploit its own minorities. The supervision of our federal government ought to prevent that.

On the issue of Negro middle-class employment in the urban bureaucracies, one must argue that the price is too high. It is these bureaucracies which now stand in the way of progress, of change and reconstruction. There is no vital connection between middle-class economic status and jobs in government. There is no reason to suppose that real local government might

---

[18] Irving Kristol, "After Decentralization, What?" *The Public Interest* (Spring 1968).

not be able to offer as many functional positions serving concrete community needs at a fair recompense. This statement does not preclude the opportunity for black people to compete with whites on the state and national level. A healthy local life in education, business, and industry ought to provide enough capable black candidates to eliminate the "window-dressing" or "token" Negro, whose lack of qualifications are often overlooked to give the appearance of integration.

In sum, it is our contention that the equality of the black man will not have been secured just because he is statistically integrated into our society. We have argued that a truer measure of equality will have been achieved, wherever it is practically possible in areas of Negro concentration, where the necessary institutional facilities will be centered in the community and be manned by black Americans. The schools will offer curricula not only partaking of the universal standards of knowledge of the Western world, but also of the cultural and historical experiences unique and special to the Negro. Finally, we would expect that the pride in real and competitive achievement and differentiation that could be obtained within the black community would do more in the long run to dissolve the ultimate psychosocial restraints of miscegenation and allow black and white to mix or not as freely as oriental and white do today.

John Oliver Killens has expressed it thus:

> My fight is not "for" racial sameness but for racial equality and "against" racial prejudice and discrimination. I work for the day when my people will be free of the racist pressures to be "white like you"; a day when "good hair" and "high yaller" and bleaching cream and hair-straighteners will be obsolete. What a tiresome place America would be if freedom meant we all had to think alike and be the same color and wear the same gray flannel suit. [19]

The Latin Minorities

The language dimension in the Puerto Rican, Cuban, and Mexican minorities significantly attenuates the complication of race with regard to their continued existence and cultural autonomy. The black man was shorn of his African heritage by

[19]John Oliver Killens, *New York Times Magazine*, June 7, 1964. Copyright © 1968 by the New York Times Company. Reprinted by permission.

slavery. What is left of his culture is a product of Southern apartheid. This in no way minimizes its significance or possibility for development. Three hundred years produces a rich enough store of tradition and self-definition for any people. Yet because the Negro, in spite of occasional Afro-American infatuations, is still an island in a sea of white, he is suspended between two antithetical goals, one, that of building a truly multidimensional cultural autonomy, the other integration and racial annihilation. Neither of these goals, much to the befuddlement of both black and white, seems possible soon.

The Latin minorities have several great advantages that can lead them to a real and enduring pluralism within the political context of our society. First, they inhabit geographical areas in which they constitute a majority (Mexicans in southern Texas, New Mexico, and Arizona, where they are in addition close to Mexico), or in which they are large minorities. For those Latin Americans such as the Puerto Ricans in New York or the Cubans in Florida, home is also close by. Indeed the traffic between Puerto Rico and New York is continuous. At the same time the American Negro has remained and will remain a stranger in Africa.

Through the traditional American educational philosophy, an attempt has been made to shear the Spanish culture from Latin American youngsters. In New York City, teachers were forbidden to speak Spanish to Puerto Rican students; in Texas special preschool programs were given in English to children of Mexican-American families whose Texas roots went back several hundred years. In New York the educational results were disastrous. In Texas children attained barely a minimal acquaintance with English before eagerly returning permanently to their Mexican American neighborhoods, rebuffed by the school and shorn of opportunities to advance educationally.

The treatment of these minorities has typified the arrogant prejudices both of the educational establishment and the dominant Anglo-Saxon political officialdom which it served.[20] The myth which was offered to rationalize a brutal and insensitive educational policy was the quasi-official status of English as a national language, and the consequent view that the Anglo-

[20]See the NEA indictment of education of Mexican-Americans in the Southwest issued in August 1966.

Saxon culture was the "American" culture, necessary to bind
our political and social fabric into one unified polity. But of
course this is philosophical nonsense. It is a nightmarish totalitarian dream to envision one homogeneous culture in a nation
as large as ours. Also, the view that unity, cooperation, and
peace depend upon homogeneity of culture is historically sus-
pect. Our bloodiest conflict, the Civil War, was fought by linguistic and racial brothers. We have fought two wars against our
English first cousins and two more against our Germanic second
cousins.

The educational ideology we have espoused—linguistic and
cultural orthodoxy within the public schools—is akin to that
which forced the Catholic to establish a parochial school system
in the mid nineteenth century. In spite of the gradual self-
consciousness of their intrinsic cultural dignity among Spanish
citizens, and because of their financial inability to leave the
public schools, the results will probably not be as schismatic.
Our proximity to Mexico and our need for Mexico's friendship
will likely cause Washington to appreciate more the inevitable
call for assistance by these minorities against the pressures of
repressive state and local educational authorities.

One has only to travel to the American Southwest to see the
powerful transformative qualities of the Spanish culture. Here
the harsh mechanical technology of the Anglo-Saxon American
has been softened, humanized, and even made intimate and
personal. The architecture, the clothing, the style of personality
and work habits, the softer accents and drawls have mellowed
the machine. In America, these geographic areas are the best
example of the nondiscursive life symbols. If given a minimal
opportunity to persevere, these symbols can interpenetrate and
enrich a quantitatively oriented and aggressive horde of newcomers. The fortune for the Southwest lies in its relatively slow
development; the frenetic ructions of the North have been
bypassed in favor of more natural humanizing of techniques,
making the task more man sized. This process of humanization
will occur in the North, but the pain of reform will be far
greater because the results of this unnatural one-sidedness are
more far-reaching.

Disregarding the growing political awareness of Spanish-
American citizens and their indisputable abilities to institution-

alize their cultural values, we already see an Anglo-Saxon majority largely Latinized, in their predelictions for Mexican foods, clothes, festivals, even use of Spanish language. It is safe to say, especially after consulting the society pages, that as the Spanish community develops educationally, socially, and politically, within the context of a mixed culture, miscegenation will occur more and more frequently. Already the indigenous universities have developed strong concentrations in the various specialties of Hispano-American culture. The sightlines are definitely South of the border, rather than to the North or the old South.

It is hardly possible, given the geographic, historic, and demographic situation in Latin-American areas, that the linguistic and cultural erosion experienced earlier by twentieth-century minority groups will befall the Spanish minorities. This prediction is made with the expectation well in mind that their social and economic conditions will rise to a level of parity with the majority culture.

Educationally a sharp and more general change is necessary. Another example of our arrogant treatment of minorities is the Indian, now receiving belated historical recognition. Whether it is the isolation of the Indian in his residential state and in federal Indian schools or preschool "anglicizing" in Texas, the practices are recidivistic. No matter that both Mexican and Indian were the indigenous peoples by some hundreds if not thousands of years. Let us put aside the issues of justice, democracy, and tolerance. Practically, it has been found that the suppression of the home and community culture of these people and the attempt to impose English and other accompanying external values have traumatized the children, made them hateful and sullen, and sterilized all possibilities of the growth of a free intelligence.[21] We cannot blame the well-intentioned middle-class white American teachers for the lack of understanding that causes this, for we train Anglo-Saxon teachers to understand the culture of others in order to give these students "our" education. A child should be taught by educated adults of his own cultural background and in the language in which his self-identification has been made.

---

[21] Ruth Landis, *Culture in American Education* (New York: John Wiley & Sons, Inc., 1965).

Language is the key here. It is a myth to think that only English is the language of the intelligent, yet this is our implicit message. It is likewise wrong to assume that a child will learn English only if it is taught to him in school as his first language. Just the opposite is true. Ignore his language of birth and he will always repress his linguistic intelligence in English. Use Spanish as a first language and offer English for its practical economic and social utility, and the practical Latin will utilize it with alacrity. For as his educated intelligence grows in the native tongue, his capacity to expand his consciousness to the other tongue grows. Yet his will is unimpaired.

If one were Machiavellian one would advise those in power who would repress this minority to continue their advocacy of the majority culture in the schools. For under these conditions the Spanish or Indian child would surely not learn or advance socially, economically, or politically. On the other hand, the resultant atrophy, hatred, and frustration engendered by insisting on an English curriculum would eventually breed its own unique problems. The growing political power of the Latin minorities will, fortunately, preclude this eventuality.

Philosophically, we insist that the existence of a political community involves no intrinsic demand for its cultural purity, or that minorities either resign from the political community or surrender their language and culture. And at the same time we must urge that within the larger national community there be room for self-governing, self-maintaining culturally unique groups with the right to demand of their membership appropriate behaviors. In our cities and towns this is not practically possible on a large scale. What we say is that there should be room in this growing synthetic Anglo-Mexican cultural environment for a variety of patterns, accents, and choices, for Mexican, Anglo-Saxon, Indian, mixed, to live together or separately in peace.

We ought not view the intrinsic demands of the Latin Americans exclusively as a search for private fulfillment. The existence of this minority in a state of health and vigor constitutes an important resource for the wider culture. As a separate center of value it can be a hindrance to any one of the many kinds of totalitarianism that may arise. Political leaders who are not only representative of the mass of men but who are responsible members of a subculture are less likely to duplicate the authoritarian, hypnotic, and charismatic leaders exemplified in more extreme political situations. Wherever there is concern for balance of powers, beyond the formal and structural legalistic sense of the Constitution, these durable limits exist on the extreme exercise of power.

In education, where the issue of creating a healthy, responsibly rational human being is central, the Spanish-speaking minority may teach us much. Its distinctiveness, unconcern for integration, its self-satisfaction and moral fulfillment while living on an economic level that equals in "deprivation" other minorities are factors that bear consideration. The Latin American is proof that happiness is not togetherness and that America is not wholly a society unified by chain drugstores.

The Mexican American of the Southwest is on the average very, very poor. But he ought not be considered deprived, or demoralized. Even in his poverty he exemplifies an inner contentment and dignity which economic status cannot touch. Thus, as yet in poverty, the Latin American can wait, law-abiding, hospitable, rich in sensory involvement and human association. In this he can perhaps be somewhat disdainful of the convulsive escalator the Anglo climbs in his journey to nowhere in particular.

The Practical Test

Just as American education absorbs one culturally diverse population, it finds new potentially indigestible groups to assimilate. Perhaps, as the Europeans learned long ago, the smoothest long-term solution lies in giving minorities the right to develop an educational program which will accommodate their own needs with those of the larger society. The dialectic between the universal and the plural is a delicate one and cannot be resolved through any all encompassing principle. It must be worked out from generation to generation and in the context of the day.

The only test of a successful cultural group can be a practical, functional one. Do the people live together harmoniously? Does the society advance and profit both culturally, economically, and scientifically from the various cultural ingredients existing in any one era? Does each group do its share? Our educational system ought not be empowered to establish as orthodox what kinds of knowledge in the nondiscursive areas of culture are suitable for the construction of a human being. These various solutions must be won by the minority groups themselves. They should develop their own curricula, choose teachers from their own groups. Yet they must reserve part of the educational enterprise to those skills conducive to a peaceful national and international life.

There are numerous minorities throughout our society—the Zuni Indians of New Mexico, the Cajuns of Louisiana, the Amish of Pennsylvania. Our educational ideal, if democratically conceived, will allow each of these groups as much freedom as is needed to establish its cultural integrity and at the same time construct a social and intellectual purview which harmonizes with the other members of our society and the broader trends of thought and action throughout the world. The theme of education ought now to be equality in difference.

CURRICULAR ISSUES

The Progressive Curriculum

Our views of curriculum have been so long couched in terms of the Darwinian doctrine—in its most biologically survivalistic interpretation of culture—that we have been blinded to the diverse possibilities in the social use of knowledge. Education is useful for more than problem solving or advancing society technologically. A curriculum should represent the system of symbolic meanings by which a child is inducted into his culture. Most typically it presents the accumulated wisdom of society; it sensitizes the child to the various areas of experience that each culture deems important.[22] At the same time the curriculum is the intellectual vehicle that advances the child from those intimate familial and common-sense meanings to wider sets of values. It helps him to function within the given sets of contemporary symbols; it invites him to explore in a creative manner the open vistas of symbolic meaning that are contained in every cultural context. A curriculum cannot rationally perpetuate a

[22] Philip H. Phenix, *Realms of Meaning* (New York: McGraw-Hill Book Company, 1964), p. 267.

system of symbols that is not only *not* predicated on the cultural life the child has experienced in his formative years but is wholly incommensurable with it.

It is true that the progressives disclaimed curricula that were abstract, artificial, and unrelated to the experiences of the child. The child-centered curriculum, with its emphasis on problem solving, core curricula, and the project method, attempted to relate learning to life. Yet these efforts resulted in little more than a shallow interpretation of life experiences derived from the biosocial intellectual proclivities of the day. It was useful, however, in toppling or destroying the older absolutistic conception of knowledge. The practical application sought in the progressive curriculum was as much a caricature of social experience as existed in the epistemology it replaced.

Culture and Science

Certainly the transformation of rationality from an inert ceremonial possession to a dynamic functioning tool for enhancing social life is as genuine a goal of a curriculum as any that might be devised today. It is a mistake to believe that a secular respect for reason can be cultivated and sustained in a valuational, philosophical, or metaphysical vacuum. Science and the scientific method are never entirely freed from their nondiscursive cultural foundations. They were created as the natural outgrowth of a set of symbolic values that were deeply felt reflections of that environment. While the seventeenth century (when modern science was created) was an era of rapid social change, the changes in our own time are no less radical. The need to root our sense of social and scientific criticism in a broad philosophical vision is as vital now for the cultivation of the scientific spirit.

Knowledge as we know it is a product of human society, if not of a class or ideology.[23] The broad expansion of Western society has shown that the discursive quality of thought can coexist with the symbolic particularities within each of the Western subcultures, indeed that it thrives on cultural differ-

---

[23] See Karl Mannheim, *Ideology and Utopia* (New York: International Library of Psychology, Philosophy and Scientific Method, 1936), an insight ultimately derived from Marx' views of the class origins of knowledge and education.

entiation. Perhaps the greatest mystery educational philosophers and theorists must probe is the process by which a child is
enabled to participate in the creative recreation and development of various orders of symbolic meaning. We know that all
creative thinkers have delved into intuitive sources of meaning
not yet discursively enough explicated to confront their doubts
and questions concerning the existing intellectual ordering of
experience.[24] If they had not genuinely felt sources of personal
experience, this hypothetical recreation of ideas could not be
effected. Today, the culturally based perception of the creative
individual is being vitiated by the monolithic qualities of our
technological world and replaced by the facile analysis of a
contemporary scholasticism that affects all areas of creative
thought today, discursive and nondiscursive.[25]

Curricula can hardly be culturally neutral if they are to
perform their intended function. As a consequence, we should
neither expect to see nor attempt to build a curriculum in any
area of experience that would be universally applicable or appropriate for all cultural settings. Mathematics and physics, in
their logical structure, transcend the particular cultures of the
West and join man in an increasingly universal set of meanings.
But this fact should not blind us to the historic creative contributions to science made by the various national schools of
physics of Western Europe.

The touchstone of any theory in the scientific realm is its
amenability for testing experimentally or experientially at some
point in its theoretical structure.[26] Certainly the technological
derivatives of Western theoretical science work equally well in
the Soviet Union, Japan, or the United States. However, the
theoretical approaches to all the scientific disciplines will be
varied. There is as yet no one system of universal laws that can
subsume all the aspects of experience under one logically derived structure of ideas. Even during the late nineteenth century
under the hegemony of Newtonian mechanics there was a vari-

[24] See Arthur Koestler, *The Act of Creation* (New York: Macmillan
Company, 1964).
[25] Thomas Munro, "Recent Developments in Aesthetics in America,"
ACLS Newsletter (February 1964), pp. 1-13; also E. Gellner, *Words and
Things* (Boston: Beacon Press, 1959).
[26] Albert Einstein, reply to Percy Bridgman, in Paul A. Schilpp (ed.),
Albert Einstein (New York: Tudor Publishing Co., 1951), p. 679.

ety of approaches to physical theory, with logical and mathematical technique being favored in France while more pictorial
models in the physical realm were favored by the English. [27]
Even in the philosophy of mathematics, certain schools have
developed different interpretations such as the logistic, inten-
tionistic and formalistic positions concerning the foundations of
the discipline. [28] In physics, in our own time, the intensely
philosophical proclivities of Austro-German educated physicists
such as Max Planck, Albert Einstein, and Ernst Mach contrast
with the more empirical and experimentally oriented physics of
the English-speaking nations.

Likewise during the nineteenth century, first the French,
then the English, and then the Germans dominated the physical
sciences. [29] Why this occurred is difficult to ascertain. Certainly
a way of looking at the world is determined by one's own
nationality as well as by the unique personal abilities of individuals. This variety in points of view in physics and chemistry was
reflected in the schools. [30] The more Western culture loses its
distinctive foci, the more probable that the stimuli of differing
schools and perspectives will also be lost and the tremendous
bursts of creative effort sustained by the kind of chain reaction
we have seen occur in differing communities will be replaced by
a bland cultural and intellectual atmosphere.

The educational journey that takes us from the particulars
(varied schools of thought) to the general (theoretical results)
does concentrate on a consensus of knowledge as regard man's
universal experiential categories. However, the existence of
varied cultural paths on which we travel toward this consensus

[27] Pierre Duhem, *The Aim and Structure of Physical Theory* (Princeton, N.J.: Princeton University Press, 1954), p. 55.
[28] Ernst Cassirer, *The Philosophy of Symbolic Forms*, trans. Ralph
Manheim (New Haven: Yale University Press, 1953), Vol. 3, p. 378.
Cassirer contrasts the mathematical realism of Newton, Mill, and Russell
with the more symbolic views of Leibnitz and Hilbert.
[29] John T. Merz, *History of European Thought in the Nineteenth
Century*, Vol. I (London: W. Blackwood and Sons, 1907-1914), passim.
[30] H. T. Pledge, *Science Since 1500* (New York: Harper & Row, Publishers) has traced the development of science in Europe in the seventeenth
and eighteenth centuries in terms of its development around one school
(university) or city in the various states. A constant cross-fertilization of
ideas from the different schools always caused the center to shift from
generation to generation, century to century.

provides the hope for new renovations in the edifice of knowledge. Here differences en route become important for curricular theorists.

Even in the United States, where differing geographical, cultural, and religious groups distinguish themselves—admittedly in an attenuated cultural form—there are possibilities for more cultural heterogeneity, given a philosophical reacquaintance by the groups with the meaning of pluralism. Thus, though we hope that Afro-American, Jew, Puerto Rican, and Georgian can agree on the facts leading to the quantum theory, we would hope that each group would have enough distinctiveness in its curricular programs that the approach might reflect slight differences in the perspective on this theory. These differences might be manifested in its mathematical representation, its experimental procedures, its particular philosophical and logical status within the broader dimensions of physics, or in its wider metaphysical significance for a theory of nature or knowledge. The logic of proof might be the same, but how we view the logic could be quite interesting and creative. Wherever different groups of men gather to solve a particular problem, they invariably come up with slightly different approaches and possibly even different answers. This happens in universities of similar cultural orientation, but it is more likely to happen in those that represent different philosophical and cultural points of view.

As stated above, the differing contexts from which knowledge is produced and the varying experiential background of scientists have provided the sources for that persistent intuitive sense of appropriateness by which every great scientific mind has held to a hypothesis that at one time or another overstepped the existing canons of truth. The stubbornness of vision that enabled a Kepler, Galileo, Newton, Pasteur, or a Darwin to resist institutionalized orthodoxy is a result of the pluralism and decentralization in culture that Western society has permitted. Heretics have a much more difficult time today. One must not be swayed by the undemocratic political and economic structure of Europe between 1600 and 1900. One of the most important elements of freedom—to think—in this cultural and intellectual realm was allowed relatively free compass. The twentieth century has made perhaps a greater exchange of freedoms than it is aware of.

Epistemology and Curriculum Construction

Our philosophical perspective presents a theoretical problem for curriculum planning: the balancing of the two ends of the epistemological spectrum. Traditionally, educational visions that have attempted to preserve the cultural outlook of a special group have generally neglected the needs for social harmony and a respect for the more universal vision of knowledge. This is especially true of those semischismatic religious groups in the United States that have attempted to separate themselves from our dominant technological and economic value system. The opposite extreme is the curriculum whose epistemological paradigm is the physical sciences. Here the attempted reification of the universal ideal in a national curriculum in all subject matter areas would tend to subvert and sterilize individual experience.[31]

Experience cannot be categorized in terms of exclusive plural and universal modes. Laying aside the variable of culture for the moment, we can study merely the physical and organic environment to find diverse intellectual and therefore curricular vectors. The disciplines of geology, zoology, and botany are examples. There are general laws in each discipline under which every particular example can be subsumed and logically related in principle. This is a basic criterion of every science. But in each ecological and geographical area the particular examples by which the general principle is illuminated must be taken from the surroundings.

An educational effort that does not include the specific concrete diversity of things as an example of the unity of theory does not serve its intellectual purposes. Presumably, all throughout the civilized community, geology, zoology, and botany curricula will be similar as well as different. To publish and utilize one text to serve a nation as large and as varied as the United States would be educationally deceitful. Yet this is a pervasive characteristic of texts in these fields.

---

[31] Admiral Hyman Rickover in his various writings, *Education and Freedom* (New York: E. P. Dutton and Co., Inc., 1959), *Swiss Schools and Ours: Why Theirs Are Better* (New York: Little, Brown and Company, 1962), *Education For All Children: What We Can Learn From England* (Washington, D.C.: U.S. Government Printing Office, 1963), has advocated a national curriculum.

In literature we can identify several universal patterns of expression, poetry and fiction, for example. Within the major examples taken from all civilizations, we develop different analytical techniques as part of various curricular approaches. We could study the formal elements of structure or we could study the substantive content of these works, their subject matter. But certainly we could not argue the esthetic qualities of each example unless we knew the varied languages and even here the classification of literary works in terms of esthetic success is hazardous enough within the cultural community to whom they were addressed.

The novel as it originated in Western Europe, however, is part of our heritage. In this sense structure, subject matter, and esthetic impact are made more easily available to us. Yet even here it is difficult to believe that translations of *Crime and Punishment, Don Quixote,* or *Madame Bovary* can render to students an understanding of the inner spirit of the work that is naturally communicated to the reader in the mother tongue.

The American novel is a more complicated example. It is meaningfully American only to the extent that it represents the American New Englander, Negro, Jew, Irish, or Deep Southerner. It depends on who is reading Edwin O'Connor, Bernard Malamud, or William Styron. These works are written in one language, yet who could doubt that the young of Irish, Jewish, or Southern background would derive more of the inner esthetic impact of the novel because of their ethnic or regional tradition? Yet the novel is broader than New York or Virginia, Boston or Texas. It is a great form within which the pluralistic dimension finds a varied but natural embodiment.

While there are symbolic areas of communication and learning that are relatively limited in their social reference to particular communities, there are other subject matter disciplines which as presently constituted demonstrate dual uses. In language, as we have noted, literature and poetry reflect unique cultural facets of life. Yet language studied for communication should be as universal as possible (Esperanto and Interlingua) or at least represent a national political entity. Thus our minority groups ought but should not be required to learn English. This is further complicated by the fact that there are all sorts of colloquial and vernacular usages to language that further different human needs. These are the varied Bronx and Brooklyn accents of the New Yorker, the Texan and Georgian drawl, and the New England twang in this supposedly uniform language. Those spoken versions often find eventual exemplification in the literature of the area and quite possibly contribute to the continuous changes to be found in the formalized written and spoken national language. It is difficult to determine how an educational enterprise might balance the various centripetal and centrifugal forces that act upon language. But every curriculum should directly confront these polar tendencies in language, as natural embodiments of human symbolic perception.

The social sciences, especially history, can be placed logically between the extremes of the nondiscursive arts and the universal logic of mathematics and the physical sciences. That there are numerous dimensions to history is obvious. But the need to teach histories and not history is not so obvious. The larger philosophical and historical dimensions of natural and human evolution apply to all of us. But there are special cultural histories wherein groups could evaluate their past as an aid in directing their future. We should have the opportunity of reflecting on the past to see man's multidimensional divergencies as well as his unities.

The teaching of history needs to be relieved of its absolutistic claims. The various cultural and philosophical interpretations of history might be presented as an alternative to a philosophy of one objective pattern of truth buttressed by supposedly hard empirical facts. A history of the United States written from the standpoint of the experience of the black American would be an important curricular addition to American education. [32] When we add to this problem of histories the current need to see our own national heritage and destiny in the light of a world increasingly committed to international social, political, and economic arrangements, we can easily see the centrality of this discipline.

Cassirer saw in history the means by which man could become attuned to the universal by truly understanding the ulti-

[32] J. H. Clarke (ed.), *William Styron's Nat Turner* (Boston: Beacon Press, 1968) is a good example of the kinds of historical and curricular debates that can occur when black men fight against the white man's interpretation of one of their culture heroes.

mate particular, himself:

> Art and history are the most powerful instruments of our inquiry into human nature. What would we know of man without these two sources of information? We should be dependent on the data of our personal life, which can give us only a subjective view and which at best are but the scattered fragments of the broken mirror of humanity. To be sure, if we wished to complete the picture suggested by these introspective data we could appeal to more objective methods. We could make psychological experiments or collect statistical facts. But in spite of this our picture of man would remain inert and colorless. We should only find the "average" man—the man of our daily practical and social intercourse. In the great works of history and art we begin to see, behind this mask of the conventional man, the features of the real, individual man. In order to find him we must go to the great historians or to the great poets—to tragic writers like Euripides or Shakespeare, to comic writers like Cervantes, Molière, or Laurence Sterne, or to our modern novelists like Dickens or Thackeray, Balzac or Flaubert, Gogol or Dostoievski. Poetry is not a mere imitation of nature; history is not a narration of dead facts and events. History as well as poetry is an organon of our self-knowledge, an indispensable instrument for building up our human universe.[33]

We have referred to a polarity in knowledge between the universal and the particular forms of knowing; it is not a sharp antithesis. One might envision this logical structure of the orders of cultural symbolism as a series of concentric circles issuing from the center toward wider and wider theories and referents. There are some areas of cultural expression that seem to be located at either the center or at the periphery. Those in between look both inward and out. The health of any society lies in cultivating the whole rather than subsuming important and obvious areas of cultural experience to logics drawn not from their own inner character but from inappropriate epistemological models whose main virtue is their great current attractiveness. The physical sciences, indeed all of discursive reason, are aids in the development of the personal qualities of cultural life. They heighten man's awareness and they sharpen the formal and structural elements in the various artistic and nondiscursive symbolic pursuits.

At the same time, cultural pluralism in society provides rich

[33] Ernst Cassirer, *An Essay on Man* (New Haven: Yale University Press, 1962), p. 206.

ground for the intellectual imagination from which new creative envisionments are to come. The deeper and more varied is man's psychic and cultural life, the more conducive it becomes for those formidable achievements in science and philosophy by which we have measured the greatness of men. One need only examine the historic eras of greatness to note the balance achieved in all areas of cultural life. The exhilarating rapidity with which changes occur today has disturbed the natural balance between the diverse experiences of social existence. We need to restudy the inner structure of each of the symbolic forms, both in the school and in life in general, so that all may contribute to the enhancement and harmony of man's intellectual needs.

IS PUBLIC EDUCATION PRACTICAL?

The choices that are available to us today, given the dynamics of our society, make it difficult to envision a pluralistic alternative. The structure of social meanings is organized in such a way that the *leitmotifs* of unification and integration provide the rationale to sustain the system. Indeed, the life symbols of economic affluence can only be supported by the overwhelming commitment of an ever-increasing number of people to the current economic structure of the organized system.

As long as the present value system satisfies the external expression of the populace's needs, a pluralist's demurral can only be academic. The moral apathy, the corruption and dishonesty, the lack of a commitment to a view of life deeper than the adolescent thirst for gadgetry may be perturbing qualities in contemporary life, but they are mere motes in the eye of society; they hardly touch the contemporary concerns of man. The swift pattern of technological change continues to provide a glittering façade of perceptual stimulation. Pluralism in culture, as it has existed for centuries in the historical traditions of Western society, seems to be an anachronism, a murmur from the past.

In the long run, man will demand his natural rights and the presently constituted system will wither and disintegrate. The deceptiveness of the mass-persuasion techniques and the shallowness of the symbolic edifice of contemporary value and meaning will contribute to the withdrawal of social assent first by the young and then by all. Let us hope that there will be living cultural alternatives, embodiments of a philosophical value system that could supplant the former symbol structure with a minimum of dislocation.

Under the present circumstances, it is doubtful that our public educational system will provide leadership for postulating alternative intellectual and social values. Schools from nursery to graduate level have been drawn into the contemporary structure of symbolic meanings. The search for democracy, which the schools have pursued as an independent value having a unique and transcendental educational status, has been surrendered for a fragmented set of goals all geared toward serving the economic symbols of our society. As we noted earlier, questions of human existence, of democracy, of intelligence and reason have been set aside as being academic anachronisms in favor of the easily attainable goals expressed by such educational writers as Kerr, Conant, and Keppel.

The leaders in the profession in the various organizations of the National Education Association are preoccupied with extinguishing any controversies concerning values. If there are disagreements, they are of the organizational type, such as the NEA versus AFT (American Federation of Teachers). The most prestigious position to which an educator can aspire is in educational administration, in which the tasks are organizational and manipulative, external to the basic intent of the educational process.

It is perhaps understandable that those in public education are fearful of philosophical controversies such as those that existed during the progressive era. As a result, the schools have taken an increasingly uncontroversial stand in their curricular and pedagogical proposals. A nondenominational, culturally neutral approach to education has made it possible to utilize the same curricular materials in all parts of our nation. Were it possible to eliminate geographical diversities—which give rise to differentiating social qualities such as Southern, Western, New England, urban, rural, religion, social status, and race—educators would no doubt eagerly accept the opportunity with alacrity. Even the image of foreign peoples presented in our texts is one that is watered down so that the student can imbibe it in terms that are completely commensurable with his own experience. Else a few faces are darkened in the name of democracy and reality. Little mystery, novelty, or foreignness is tolerated in the public school. We fear the real differences of symbolic values.

Public education today serves a different function than it has in the past. For over a century the public schools were a bastion of the democratic vision. They are hardly that today. Not only do they promulgate programs that subtly undermine many democratic freedoms, but they no longer contribute to the process of social and class egalitarianism that they helped succor in preceding generations. The existence of universal public education is no guarantee today that a child will be able to free himself from the social and economic degradation that still afflicts a large proportion of Americans. We have mastered and perfected the art of constructing external façades that give the illusion but not the substance of democracy.

There is little hope that evolutionary change can redeem public education. Its involvement in the life symbolism of our contemporary culture is complete. However, we must make use of the few opportunities we have. Gladys Wiggin, in a recent history of American education, described the role nationalities have had in building schools that reflected the diversity of values.[34] And while most of her study was concentrated on the latter part of the nineteenth century and the early decades of the twentieth century, she notes that a residue of agitation for ethnic, cultural, and national values in the schools still remained in 1962. Yet because of the continued efforts of both the schools and our dominant ideology of assimilation, these demands for incorporation of the ethnic cultural values into the schools have steadily waned.

Today, possibilities such as these account for only a very small sector of the potential for pluralism. Wherever one travels in the United States, one can see citizens who are concerned to set themselves off from others to accentuate not only their geographical differences, but cultural qualities as well. The substance of the desire for differentiation is there, whether in arts and crafts, cuisine, culture, or just friendliness.[35]

[34] Gladys A. Wiggin, *Education and Nationalism* (New York: McGraw-Hill Book Company, 1962).

[35] According to the Modern Language Association, there are, in addition to a large number of people who are to some extent bilingual, some twenty million persons living in America whose native tongue is not English.

Though the yearning to be individual is too deeply rooted to be eliminated, it seems doomed to peripheral manifestations as long as opportunity is lacking for a broad-ranging commitment to values that depart from the present commercialized society. The values must touch each man uniquely and deeply and must come from his own experiential environment. It is doubtful that the needs for such a cultural venture would germinate in the public schools. It must be reiterated that richness of cultural existence can be stimulated through an educational system, but this education must invoke the support of the community it serves. For such an educational achievement we may have to search outside our public schools.

THE RELIGIOUS DIMENSION

Subsidized Pluralism

One area in our social life has, to some extent, resisted the integrating tendencies in our culture. Pluralism still has a place within the religious life of our society. Externally at least people respect the varied modes of spiritual rejuvenation that are still extant. This is appropriate philosophically, as innumerable scholars have attested. Myth and religion represent the basic areas of symbolic expression in which the deepest feelings and emotions of men are manifested.

The relative vigor of religious differentiation in our times—despite the fact that for the most part the masses have lost a metaphysics of belief—is an important support to the symbolic philosophy. Religious life satisfies the need for community life and participation in shared experiences by people brought together through tradition, historical association, acceptance of inner personal or moral values, or through a church that represents some of the more transcendental mysteries of existence. In addition to the human fellowship that binds men together through this commitment to shared experience, some of the more sacred human moments can be celebrated in the mutually accepted symbols of religion—birth, baptism, puberty rites, marriage, and death.

Thus it is that today, in our culture, much intense controversy is being raised over religion and education. There are those, in this case predominantly Catholic, who wish to exercise their rights to educate their children in the values of their faith. They resent the debilitating double taxation now imposed. They would have government, either state or national, aid them financially in exercising their choice in the education of their children.

A few years ago a symposium concerned itself with this issue of subsidized pluralism.[36] In the process of the discussion, many important aspects of pluralism were raised, among them the relationship of state to individual, universal values of unity versus separation and apartheid. It is unfortunate that the discussion was largely framed in terms of subsidized religious pluralism rather than a more broadly defined pluralism. However, as such, it provides a sufficiently developed context within which the issues broached could be extended to larger areas of pluralistic concern.

Robert Creegan, one of the participants, set forth the pluralistic argument as follows:

> To subsidize students for education in schools of their choice is, in fact, to subsidize a variety of public and private schools, albeit indirectly. Thus, the method of subsidy is secondary to the basic principle of pluralism. Monopoly is the real enemy. The rights of competing philosophies, professions, religions, and ethnic interest must not be abrogated for the benefit of a bureaucracy in education. The function of the state in education is one of guidance, inspection, and arbitration. Pluralism rules against dictatorship. It detests monopoly for monopoly's sake. It celebrates the protection of group interests, as well as of individual interests, by the liberal state. . . .
>
> A pluralist does not condemn the public schools, but does argue in the strongest terms that citizenship in a free society implies common assent only to certain constitutional principles. We are not concerned with the question whether John Dewey offers better educational ideals than does Albert Schweitzer or St. Thomas Aquinas or any other great thinker. The question of importance to pluralists is whether any total philosophy should be prescribed for the training of all teachers or for the management of all tax-supported schools. We believe that monopoly in applied educational philosophy is totalitarian in spirit. Such monopoly in tax-supported education is also unconstitutional in principle, as far as the U.S. and its political postulates are con-

---

[36] Joshua Fishman (ed.), "Subsidized Pluralism in American Education," *School and Society* (May 23, 1959).

cerned in this dispute. In addition, a monopoly will lower the quality of education.

A way should be found to subsidize from tax sources the education of individuals in schools and colleges representing differing educational principles and procedures, but unified through common adherence to constitutional principles and common acceptance of segments of the curriculum mandated by public educational authorities for the public welfare. Public inspection, no doubt, would be necessary to enforce these provisos. It also seems reasonable to mandate the teaching of pluralistic principles in all tax-aided schools, not in the sense of indoctrination, but rather in that of explanation. Some understanding of the principles of pluralism should be required of teachers and of students, at least of certain age groups, in all schools receiving any type or amount of assistance from public tax sources.[37]

With the exception of the Catholic, Charles Donahue, the participants disagreed with Creegan's plea.[38] Their concerns ranged from Richard Plaut's fears for a return to segregation to the concern for intergroup relations expressed by Marshall Sklare of the American Jewish Committee.[39,40] Martin Chworowski and Joshua Fishman (the latter was chairman of this University of Pennsylvania conference) expressed concern that subsidized pluralism would introduce governmental intervention into the area to produce fragmentation rather than unity. As Joshua Fishman gently phrased it:

> To subsidize diversity, to give it a financial and institutional base, would seem to most Americans like asking for trouble. Having at long last arrived at a reasonably satisfying and righteous sounding *modus vivendi*, it would seem to be discreet not to disturb it. The American tradition of compromise is an important ingredient in this approach. All problems can be solved and all contradictory views reconciled if the parties that differ will only sit down together, talk things over, and give in a little to each other. We dislike the prolongation of a public disagreement and the intemperance of diehards. Thus, though we may regret uniformity and wax nostalgic about diversity, we want our diversity

[37] Robert F. Creegan, "Quality and Freedom Through Pluralism," *School and Society* (May 23, 1959), pp. 248-249.

[38] Charles Donahue, "Religion and State Power: The American Pattern," *School and Society* (May 23, 1959), pp. 253-256.

[39] Richard L. Plaut, "The Segregational Aspects of Publicly Subsidized Pluralism," *School and Society* (May 23, 1959), pp. 251-253.

[40] Marshall Sklare, "Ethnic-Religious Groups and Publicly Subsidized Pluralism," *School and Society* (May 23, 1959), pp. 260-263.

to be sterile rather than virile. Subsidized pluralism might get out of hand.[41]

Martin Chworowski put the issue a bit more bluntly in his claim that subsidized pluralism could "lead to a kind of apartheid, or cultural parallelism in which clusters of groups gather to preserve their own identity and bring about the gradual eclipse of what started out as cultural pluralism.[42]

In fact, Chworowski warned, the involvement of government in the subsidization of pluralism, as in the schools, could increase the role of government in our lives to the detriment of individual and group freedom.

> This brings us to the basic issue. It seems that subsidized pluralism means, an enlargement of the welfare state and will increase the trend in our life towards the kind of totalitarianism which . . . has been one result of a rise of liberal individualism, which has failed to see the danger to democracy in the elimination of many voluntary associations through which individualism always has been nourished.[43]

A genuine fear was expressed in this conference of introducing government responsibility to an area that traditionally has been a province of private social enterprise. Much of this concern has an historically familiar ring. It has been evidenced in opposition to numerous governmental extensions—Social Security, labor legislation, social welfare, civil rights. And we cannot omit a more liberal concern for the resulting outcome of prior governmental interventions in education for separation. "Just as we have learned that state support of equal and separate schools only led to inequality among Negroes and whites, so subsidized cultural pluralism may lead to the liquidation of diversity and freedom.[44] If we face the unexplored practical and philosophical complexities of subsidized pluralism in the context of the present intergroup hostilities and competitions, we can understand more readily this conservative concern about governmental involvement.

---

[41] Joshua A. Fishman, "The American Dilemmas of Publicly Subsidized Pluralism," *op. cit.*, pp. 265-266.
[42] Martin Chworowski, "Subsidized Pluralism: Its Implications for Intergroup Relations," *op. cit.*, p. 259.
[43] *Ibid.*, pp. 259-260.
[44] *Ibid.*, p. 260.

Discussion

Fuller enquiry into the problem of governmental involvement in subsidized pluralism reveals philosophical issues not quite grasped by many of the participants in the symposium. We do not have a simple choice between governmentally sponsored pluralism or laissez faire exploitation by the individual of his own cultural proclivities. Rather it is a choice between governmental support of pluralism or governmental support of an official homogeneous culture. The existence of an official culture is not merely a potential threat, for it already prevails on both state and local levels. Today as always in the United States, the government has been an active subsidizer of values in education. These values have not necessarily been derived from scientific and secular humanism, as many religionists claim. Nor have they been derived from any consciously proclaimed value scheme. By vigilant supervision of the public schools, various contending groups—religious, fraternal, and patriotic—have seen to it that education has been denatured of all but the most superficial scientific values. The encounter with Dewey's instrumentalism has been a sure goad to this close supervision.

While it is true that the public schools have been deprived of consciously developed value systems because of the diverse backgrounds of the students, it is not true that the schools have been denied *any* value system. It is impossible to do away with the use of symbols in knowledge and in the structure and organization of educational activities. What has happened is that the supposedly noncontroversial subject matter areas have taken on a structural and symbolic life of their own. They represent much more than supposedly objective and noncontroversial facts of knowledge. The objectivity is, of course, spurious. This external material value schema that is here represented has been extended into all areas of the enterprise. The educational leadership has now accepted and does espouse this supposedly neutral symbolic edifice which at least has the virtue of avoiding the traditional controversial value systems.

More than once we have stated that these new values are derived from that union of naive epistemological realism and the science that feeds the materialism of our commercial society. The educational values are composed of a static set of facts to be absorbed by way of rote techniques—the mechanics of learning. Retention of these values is tested in such mass objective examinations as college boards and regents exams, which are given in an impersonal, sterile manner. (They are usually multiple-choice.) The cultural sustenance that gives broader social relevance to these examinations is derived from the symbols of success in life and the material emoluments that will accrue to the "winners."

Even with the philosophical buttressing given to the schools by our commercialized society, confidence in the anonymous world of public education has gradually lessened. The recent rapid growth of private and parochial schools in spite of double taxation has been engendered not only because of the growing affluence of our culture, but also because of parents' desire to place their children in schools in which an intimate setting of generally sympathetic values may touch the deeper cultural and personal needs of the child.

The attempts of the unifiers and integrators to reduce the educational enterprise to one structure of values in science, art, and religion result eventually in a war of values between an officially sponsored educational system financed by tax monies and a host of private educational ventures subject to the attrition of competition, inherently hostile regulation by the states, and the near-confiscatory taxation of those who send their children to private schools. Implicit here is a conflict in philosophies of human nature. It is between those who believe social life can be lived as one cultural entity and those who believe there should be sectors of private egress from the all-encompassing grasp of the organized system. From this conflict, as we have discussed above, evolves a divergence of views on the nature of democracy that must be confronted and resolved.

There is a legitimate concern over the traditional sectarian divisiveness that has inevitably entered the social scene, given the coexistence of several cultural groups. We must face the threat that fragmentation poses for the security of the democratic society. But it is not simply an issue of pluralism or unity. What might better be engaged in is an examination of the educational elements necessary for the retention of those qualities of unity historically found necessary for the cohesion and freedom of our democracy. We also need to study the academic frame in which diversity flourishes, for diversity in turn succors the inner health and productivity of the larger society.

Here again, another distinction can be helpful. That pluralism subsidized by government in the religious area "might lead to bloc voting, to splinter groups in political parties, and to religious cliques in governmental offices and business,[45] as well as class differences, racial segregation, and intergroup hostility is an important and valid concern. Perhaps government should only support those aspects of education that philosophically promote the rational capacities of man where intelligence is used in the service of the law. Those curricular areas of experience concerned with the aspects of life that unite all men—the sciences and social sciences—could be taught through a philosophy that stresses respect for and development of those secular capacities of reason that lie at the root of the search for unity in man's physical and social environment. To the extent that public or private schools achieve this, regardless of the esthetic and moral overtones that distinguish differences in method in the sciences in all societies, government should be expected to supply some subsidization.

Respect for reason and scientific method in dealing with physical, biological, and social phenomena, can occur in the context of Puerto Rican, Jewish, Mississippian, or Catholic schools. We need not fear that private and parochial schools will automatically produce a society riven by power-hungry cliques attempting to gain advantage for their own groups. By establishing philosophical guidelines for educational and social diversity, we might be able to avoid the historic pitfalls of past internecine conflict.

The search for law in man's social life has been dominated by an all-encompassing search for freedom that is compatible with all cultural frames. All that society can ask is that groups renounce the coercive use of power, especially when any one of them achieves momentary dominance. The principle we seek is one that persuades all communities to commit themselves to equality before the law and to sanction the free and full exercise of each individual's right of choice in cultural values. An even greater danger than bloc voting or religious and cultural cliques is the usurpation of power by colorless, antiseptic bureaucracies or specialists who represent nothing more humane than naked control.

45 Martin Chworowski, *op. cit.*, p. 257.

It seems evident that the government might have the obligation to guarantee that all schools in our society fulfill this demand for the development of that active quality of intelligence useful not only in contemplation and study of the inner structure of matter, but in the pursuit of principle in the study of society. To the extent that, for example, Catholic schools have failed to develop this type of social intelligence, Catholic education has effectively removed itself from its responsibilities to the larger public and therefore has abnegated its rightful demand for subsidies in this area of knowledge and curriculum.

If we assume that scientific intelligence is the highest development of a basic proclivity of human nature that seeks order, law, and principle in the realm of man's material and social environment, then state subsidization of every school promoting this end is to be recommended. It is a right that accrues to the individual partaking of the school's educational services. The recent (1968) upholding by the Supreme Court of the New York State law on loans of textbooks to parochial and private schools has stimulated the demand for more general aid, such as remedial reading and guidance services. [46]

As noted earlier, the laws of society that serve to insure men's freedom are prolegomena to the more important question of the use of this freedom. It is in the nondiscursive areas of social life that man fulfills the deeper emotive needs of life and reinforces his creative intellectual endeavors. This inevitably has consequences in the wider social community. By focusing as it does on symbolic realms of discourse whose reference is a limited and communal one, education here necessitates a distinctly pluralistic curricular as well as institutional approach. Here the Catholic, Jewish, Polish, Negro, New Mexican, Hutterite, perhaps even the "Diggers," can be educated so that they participate creatively in their own community of values and systems of meaning valuable to the individual and therefore valuable to the larger society. We would hope that in their religious concerns Catholic, Jewish, or Protestant schools would make the necessary distinctions between the logic of faith as it applies to the perennial religious qualities of transcendence, good and evil, sin and redemption, and the secular concerns of man that lie in

[46] *New York Times*, July 2, 1968.

the discursive realm. We would hope that there would be no attempt, as was once common, to apply dogmatic truths literally to such social or intellectual problems as evolutionary theory, or to social issues, such as population control.[47]

Religion has been used with less and less frequency as a basis for decision making in the public sphere since the writing of the First Amendment. The values and uses of religion today are in fact predominantly centered in the nondiscursive realm. Men still enjoy participating in the rituals of their groups. The need to distinguish like from unlike is basic. Religion also provides the locus of social action for concerned groups once a discursive intellectual decision is made.

The Southern Christian Leadership Conference under the late Martin Luther King is an example of this important facet of religion. Certainly the discursive logic of its demands for equality is based on the common fund of reason established by the canons of scientific evidence. The moral fervor, the willing commitment to action are in addition unique existential values ultimately rooted in Negro religious beliefs. While deep religious commitment is the spur to action, scientific reason has guided its decisions. That the state benefits by the teachings and associations of a religious environment cannot be doubted, as long as these functions are focused on their appropriate symbolic province.

Associated with man's religious convictions are the communal cultural values that form a constellation of harmoniously related meanings. These meanings alone present to the child a world through which he can define both his external and his internal experience. Without a community to participate in, share, and recreate this symbolic world, life has no substance; it loses its ability to build whole men and women. The minimum obligation of the larger political structure is to see that education promotes the idea of symbolic community. It is important that each person in our nation have the opportunity to become a member of a subculture. At this level, subsidization of education—private, parochial, and public—would seem to be a public obligation.

[47] The Encyclical *Humanae Vitae* of Pope Paul on this matter is an example of a philosophical obstinacy of the Church reifying itself into what may eventually be a gross historical error that the church itself will have to modify.

ETHNIC AND CULTURAL
PLURALISM IN INTERNATIONAL PERSPECTIVE

The Great Hope

Rational men view the prospect of a world community as an eventuality both necessary and inevitable. Every year that passes without bringing us closer to this goal is a year of lost opportunities and perhaps tragic and avoidable strife between members of a world community. The Utopian vision embodied in this hope is not merely an abstract desire for unification. It entails the substantive aspiration for a measure of economic and social equality within the context of a technology that is world-wide in development. As part of this dream there surely must be room for the desire that the resources nature has given to our earth be utilized for the benefit of all mankind, not just any one nation.

There are countless technicalities involved in distributing the wealth that has been and will be in the future scarcer than the masses of people demanding their share. Certainly they are manageable considering the technical advances in population control, agriculture, transportation, and communication. The visionaries of world federalism have more often than not framed their ideals in terms of political and economic unities and equalities, all very logical and reasonable extrapolations of this vision.

The Orwellian suggestion of an empowered United Nations ruling over a homogeneous world community is however ultra-Utopian. As an incomplete statement of an ideal it is perhaps reasonable. But since it does not deal with the cultural heterogeneity of mankind, except to assume that cultural heterogeneity is a product of a mixed and varied level of technological and economic advance, it is seriously deficient. It makes an assumption about man which is refuted daily, even in the industrially advanced nations of the world.

The crucial issue today is how to transfer the vast multitude of tribes or ethnic and language groups into a world community while retaining their heritage. Every culture carries with it a large number of cultural values from the past which run counter to some of the basic conditions of modern life. Not only religious beliefs, but social and political forms, rights of women, and dietary habits, of countless groups seem to defy modernity and scientific rationality.

Another nation, Mexico, having the same general developmental problem, but with a more complicated cultural, racial, and ethnic background, took a more tolerant philosophical perspective concerning the need to urge backward people into the twentieth century without violating their cultural and linguistic integrity:

> But what is still lacking, on the part of the rest of the Mexican population of Western culture, is serious thought on what the present situation of cultural, ethnic and linguistic pluralism means in the development of Mexico. When this is achieved, thanks to the information and diffusion efforts of the Indian organizations, the spontaneous help of the public can be relied upon in bringing about "mexicanization" of all those ethnic elements which until now have really been "marginal."
>
> And "mexicanization" does not mean suppressing the true values of the Indian cultures. It means only seeking the elevation of its people in those aspects in which it can be asserted that the pre-Columbian cultural survivals are harmful. With this standard, an attempt is made to transform their primitive agricultural and industrial techniques, their hygiene, economy, etc. When this is achieved, and when the ancient problems deriving from the ethnic and cultural pluralism disappear, the true cultural physiognomy of Mexico will finally appear in its fulness, enriched by the positive values, not only of the Western culture, but also by those which have been supplied by the pre-Columbian Indian cultures.[52]

On the other hand, the Brazilian scholar Gilberto Freyre takes a negative view of pluralism in Brazil. Freyre extols the "fusionism" of Brazilian culture, whereby this society so easily accepted and assimilated all types of foreign elements, racial, ethnic, cultural, and even "civilizational."

> When assimilation goes as far as to include literature of the most lyrical and intimately introspective kind, this means that Brazilians of European non-Portuguese origin are really becoming a new force in Brazilian life and culture, by the side of descendants of Portuguese, Amerindian and Negro, through old instruments of expression such as the Portuguese language and the Portuguese lyrical tradition.[53]

The Brazilian situation is of course different from the Mexican. The Portuguese are the only representatives of their lan-

[52] Miguel León-Portilla, "Ethnic and Cultural Pluralism in the Mexican Republic," *op. cit.*, p. 478.

[53] Gilberto Freyre, "Plural and Mixed Societies in the Tropics: The Case of Brazil Considered From a Sociological Point of View," *op. cit.*, p. 492.

guage tradition in the New World. To this self-consciousness of minority status is added the complicating issue of a large former Negro slave population in the impoverished Northeast provinces, in spite of the tolerant Latin attitudes towards intermarriage and social mixing between the races. These former slaves as a result carry with them more of their African cultural heritage than do most other New World Negroes. The small indigenous Indian population is not significant, but the newer and more vigorous Europeans (such as Italian or German) are a challenge to the traditional Portuguese element. One suspects Freyre's Brazilian fusionism, while far more real than in the United States, still constitutes a means for maintaining a Portuguese primacy akin to the melting-pot, Anglo-Saxon view.

Freyre's view is rather exceptional, the more typical being an appreciation of the empirical fact that people either naturally resist complete assimilation—even in the context of religious homogeneity—or are indeed able to live in virtual peace in a context of separation and pluralism. The conclusions of Francis G. Carnell's article on Burma, Thailand, and Malaya must be seen in the context of pre-1957, when this area was still free from the ideologically complicating circumstances that have engulfed it since that time.

> Despite the spate of post-war minority problems in the area, we should not be too pessimistic about the future. Taking a long view, there is something in the Southeast Asian environment which is particularly conducive both to the fusion of cultures and to the peaceful co-existence of cultures. The Southeast Asian peoples are undoubtedly amongst the most tolerant in the world. Racism, chauvinism and religious fanaticism, though not unknown, have been far less pronounced than elsewhere. Though group tensions exist, they have never led in the modern period to mass slaughter, downright persecution or the denial of human rights.[54]

This view is similar to J. S. Furnival's (in *The Tropical Far East*) that the Asiatic tropics have developed "a plural society in which different communities live side by side but separately, and have no common interest except in making money."[55]

---

[54] Frances G. Carnell, "Ethnic and Cultural Pluralism in Burma, Thailand and Malaya," *op. cit.*, p. 421.

[55] Cited by Gilberto Freyre, "Plural and Mixed Societies in the Tropics: The Case of Brazil Considered From a Sociological Point of View," *op. cit.*, p. 486.

But perhaps the most remarkable example of a group's fight
to retain its cultural identity can be found in Israel, where one
would expect a great willingness to forgo the historical accidents of differentiation in favor of a common culture.

Many of the new immigrants clung very fiercely to some
aspects of their traditions and social life and were not ready to
give all of them up. The pressure towards homogeneity only produced quite often various aspects of social disorganization, both
among adults and adolescents and children. Gradually it became
apparent that existing social groups and traditions will have to be
taken into account and some legitimate scope found for them.
This does not mean, of course, that new processes of change will
not take place, but that in this process of change some of the older
traditions will be either perpetuated or transformed, in a stable
way. It is as yet difficult to say what will be the concrete process
of selection and in which areas some basic cultural homogeneity
will develop and in which ones greater heterogeneity will prevail.
It seems that in the field of language there will develop a gradual
homogeneity and that there, Hebrew language will become, at
least in the second generation, the main common-language. The
influence of the school and the army will be decisive here. The
same will probably be true in matters of daily dress—mainly for
reasons of utility and convenience. But differences will probably
remain in patterns of festive dress. Differences will probably also
be perpetuated in the field of ritual traditions, in the field of
folk-traditions of various kinds (songs, dances, etc.). In the social
field different patterns of family life will probably remain for a
longer period than differences in the occupational field. In the
economic field itself probably various types of traditional handi-
crafts will be promoted for some time.

These are, however, mainly surmises based on the actual developing situations; it is difficult to forecast various details. But
the general patterns seem to be following these lines. Thus it can
be summarized that Israel is developing into a socially integrated
community in which there will be a large scope for cultural
pluralism in many secondary spheres.[56]

What Eisenstadt calls the secondary sphere coincides with
various nondiscursive symbolic areas of expression, more significant than the role he assigns them. Of course, to a nation in
which economic and technological advance means literally political survival, and whose unity of religion bridges the cultural
difference that the Israeli immigrants have brought with them,

---

[56] S. N. Eisenstadt, "Ethnic and Cultural Pluralism in Israel," *op. cit.*,
p. 390.

the reduction of sharp variations and the minimization of other cultural distinctions are understandable and partially validated.

Contemporary Issues

The issue of priorities is crucial to the resolution of the sometimes contradictory manifestations of social modernization and cultural self-consciousness. The most horrifying example of this dilemma is the story of Nigeria. This nation, racially homogeneous, but with vast differences in language, religion, level of civilizational sophistication, even in basic life styles, was a tribal conglomerate created for the colonial convenience of the British government. In setting Nigeria free, Britain expected that its future political influence would be determined by its success in maintaining its national viability. The subsequent massacres by the numerically superior Hausas of the North of the more energetic Christian Ibos should have dissipated that hope. The genocidal endeavors of the Muslim dominated Nigerian government against Biafra have been supported by Great Britain in the name of the preservation of national unity. But Nigeria has never been a nation in terms of tradition, culture, history. There is no rationalization for the argument that the cultural rights of a vigorous, progressive, self-conscious minority have to be sacrificed in the name of national unity (the myth of balkanization). It is a product of the mechanistic biases of our systems analysts. Culture, too, resists programming. And, at the risk of extermination, the Biafrans resisted. Their belief was that it is quite possible to attain political, economic, and social modernization within a confederation in which their identity would not be inundated. And who will deny them the validity of this demand?

These problems are not restricted to Nigeria or the Congo. Both Belgium and Canada are experiencing similar problems of material equality and cultural parity. In the case of Belgium a small, highly industrialized nation, the traditionally poorer and ignored Flemings of the North have recently benefited by a significant measure of economic advance. Flemish is a relatively minor dialect of Dutch, while the Walloons of the South authoritatively speak the French of their neighbors and coreligionists.

Belgium must face the fact that what was formerly the language of the plebeian poor is now the language of a vigorous and numerically superior proportion of the population. Can a language of the streets and villages be given equal official status on every educational level with French? The Flemings believe it is necessary for their full development. The agitation at the Catholic University of Louvain for Flemish parity was no doubt not without cause.

Can we expect any culture to maintain itself without official recognition even with a cohesive and rich communitarian folk culture? It is doubtful. It needs the full envisionment of secondary and higher education, and eventually official national use equal to French. Only then can we expect the kinds of scholarship, literature, and art that are representative of a fully realized culture. Merely because a language has traditionally been the language of the poor does not preclude its potentiality for development.

In the case of Canada, we also have an economically deprived and politically humble minority, this time French, demanding a greater level of cultural equality along with the need for economic advance. The question is not alone one of nationalism. The argument of economic and political viability is real in each national case. With Biafra, it is reasonable to expect that a tight national federation would breach the most elemental human rights of these peoples. Thus political, military, and international defences are necessary. This is not the case in Belgium or Canada, where the centralist traditions are far stronger and the peoples closely integrated for centuries. We need not fear that the French Canadians will capitulate to General DeGaulle. In Canada the demand for a true biculturalism is persuasive. The French Canadians need more French-language universities and have the right to expect that French enclaves in the English-speaking provinces of the West will be allowed to set up government supported French schools.

The issue of national unity versus cultural freedom ought never be resolved in favor of the abstraction and against the individual beings. In fact, our civilizational values will be more protected and succored in the context of pluralism of small decentralized states than in the vast, transcultural nations where technical efficiency and mechanical, police imposed unity are sure to reap their human toll.

chapter **6**

A Strategy for Change

DIALECTICAL TRENDS

The black flag of anarchism, tattered and forlorn, has flown from few citadels in the last one hundred and fifty years. The times have not favored those who advocated small governments or any other diminished institutional element of modern society. To effect a change, to slacken our involvement with great institutions and massive numbers, and to retard the expanding concentric pulsations of authority, regimentation, and inevitably uniformity, the dialectical *élan vital* of centralism must be immobilized.

But how can we effect the change? We have had our antitheses in the Fourierists, in our Brook Farms, in the Proudhons and Bakunins of the nineteenth century. In our own twentieth century, Dewey, Laski, and Kallen have been honored and forgotten. They were of little historical avail. How can we reverse a tide which has been irresistible for so long? If it is possible at all, it is only because new social conditions may now have arisen in the West that heretofore were not thought imminent.

Nothing has greater power over man than an idea, an idea that will allow him to pour his amazing reservoir of psychic energies into its fulfillment. The scientific and industrial revolutions and the social and institutional revolutions which accompanied them were the embodiment of such an idea. Its power to dominate man's sense of reality, to motivate him to act and be acted upon in a manner which surpassed and violated all prior social and moral norms is reflected in the gross evils that accompanied the process of industrialization and urbanization. The horrors of the cities from the late eighteenth century to the present were to be endured in the name of progress. And prog-

ress of course was achieved even at a price on life far in excess
of any earlier but similar historical trend. The dynamics of centralization and the symbols of universalism could not be
stemmed. They encompassed a pervasive climate of opinion,
and no institution, philosophy, or set of human rights could
stand in their way.

One can thus trace the alternations in the dialectics of
human progress since the start of civilization. From centralization to decentralization, from homogeneity to heterogeneity,
the gyrations and pulses have been manifested, for example, in
Egypt's period of unification and pyramid building and its subsequent dissolution and lengthy lapse into feudalism; in the
growth of the Roman Empire upon the political and military
failure of the disorganized and anarchic Greeks, followed in
turn by Rome's own collapse and the long "dark" era of Christian anti-institutionalism. But the cultural seeds of this era of
disorganization eventually germinated, resulting in the flourish-
ing of the Gothic, Renaissance, Baroque, and Romantic cultures
of Europe.

Perhaps we are past the apex of our enchantment with empire building, at least in Western society. The vision and purpose
of the overseers of our system are becoming increasingly ob-
scured. More and more social bills are coming due, adding to the
inertial drag. Perhaps most crucial of all, the institutional patterns which the young now inherit, which enthralled the older
generation, have a new visage. They seem like monolithic vestiges, incapable of eliciting intelligence, ardor, or idealism.

Perhaps this is an era of transition. The vision of the cyber-
netician is in eclipse. The organization men are not as assured.
From the Pentagon to the political alleys and even to the state
education departments there is less confidence in the ability to
program either institutions or people. In more colloquial terms
we can say that people no longer wish to be pushed around.
Rather there is an increasing demand for freedom of choice,
that essential morsel of man's birthright.

People are now ready to listen, especially when the call is
for autonomy, diversification, and pluralism. The mechanistic
centralists have lost their charm. The rivers and lakes are pol-
luted and dying. Our lungs gasp for clean air. Disaffection is rife
not only in the urban Negro and the radical young, but in those

of the middle class, hustling like affluent robots, yet frozen to their institutional treadmills.

However, a massive attack on the system, as now being attempted by the minority poor and the young, is out of the question. It is to be understood, but deplored. Too many people are being hurt. Even peaceful agitation, though a legitimate right that needs to be exercised, should be attempted only through the step-by-step creation of a responsive climate of opinion. For this we need a set of discrete and deliberative social and political steps that will establish the direction of change.

Some argue that the only alternative to the present system is the horse and buggy. The price of technology, they can document persuasively, is the ugly, neurotic, power-intoxicated world we live in. We have had sober warnings that those in power usually control the form as well as the content of knowledge. But it is difficult to refute the vested interests of our time. We do not want to surrender our dishwashers, hi-fi sets, or our automobiles, even in exchange for a more humane world. There are few economists who devote themselves to the practical delineation of an alternative view of social reality, J. Kenneth Galbraith being one of these few. We should be thankful for the seers such as Paul Goodman who have at least made the first tentative steps toward intellectualizing the heretofore illiberal concept of decentralization.[1]

THE NEMESIS OF POPULATION

There are social and historical grounds upon which every intellectual position either succeeds or flounders. The threat to pluralism, diversity, and decentralization is certainly the massive population explosion taking place in our century. As an example, democracy and individualism have never had a place in the densely populated river valleys of India, China, and Egypt,

[1] Paul Goodman's *People or Personnel* (New York: Random House, Inc., 1965) is an interesting example of an attempt to put into dollars-and-cents terms some of the economic as well as social waste that the system of gigantic institutions perpetuates and which are often hidden from public view. Goodman's analysis, however, is more suggestive than systematic. An important field of socially useful economic research needs to be explored here.

where the need to manage hordes of closely compacted individuals necessitated ever more regulating centralized controls. These regulations first extinguished gross cultural diversities, but ultimately they penetrated a whole range of freedoms, processes, and initiatives heretofore considered sanctified—intrinsic qualities of behavior in more loosely organized periods.

Fortunately for social stability the changes in our society have not been precipitous. Man gradually surrenders one freedom after another as he gains alternate protections and guarantees. This is usually called progress. Before long the generations have not only changed places in history; they have truly changed the qualitative structure of their lives. This is what is happening in our own era, and the changes have not been caused by technology alone. The heavy burden of more people increasingly concentrated in the great metropolitan areas has engendered hazards and fears that require control, regulation, and limitations in the sphere of personal choice and action usually not thought necessary in democracy.

While the public is only now becoming aware of this issue, foresightful groups of individuals have begun to focus seriously on this most real danger. Out of this growing concern a number of alternative suggestions has emerged: (a) equal the spiral of population growth with the expansion of food resources, mechanization, fertilizers, new strains of rice and wheat; develop mass-production techniques for providing clothing, shelter, and all the other basic necessities of life; (b) slow down the population expansion so that it gradually peaks at a level in which the ecological balance between need and availability can be maintained; (c) adjust the population according to a worldwide formula that would stipulate a propitious relationship between the numbers of people and the natural environments conducive to the peace and creative advance of all mankind in a context of plenty, equality, and diversity.

The first alternative (a) would seem to destine man for a suicidal confrontation with the unknown eventualities of the future. Fewer and fewer advocates of this position are heard from each year. The second (b) is becoming part of our conventional wisdom. It depends for its fulfillment on the voluntary use of family-planning techniques by couples interested in improving their standard of living in the context of a rapidly advancing technological economy. Even in the United States where these values and conditions are most widespread, where food and land surpluses and individual freedom still abound, the population is expected to increase indefinitely into the future. At present rates of birth and death, a population of 337 million people is now predicted for the year 2000. Those who advocate this alternative expect living space will be in surplus indefinitely, that food is no problem and pollution will somehow be contained.

The third option (c) is the one rarely heard, but which on the basis of the pluralistic position seems to be the only one that could lead to a more humanizing environment. It is true that as currently structured our society has little difficulty with gross material satisfactions, given the present technological state of our economy. However, our society is developing serious difficulties in meeting the psychic, cultural, and intellectual needs of our citizenry. It is difficult to postulate that advancing technology, more speed, more goods, even more leisure time can solve the kinds of social and ecological problems we can foresee occurring more often in the future. It is therefore doubtful that the present course will create an environment in the year 2000 that will give its citizens even as many options for choice as it did in 1900.

With merely a glance, the educational implications of an expanding population are clearly visible. An education suitable for the life style of a population of 300 to 350 million certainly cannot emphasize the qualitative individuation that has been the ostensible American educational theme heretofore. More likely it will be an education which emphasizes vocational specificity and acceptance of certain preordained patterns of behavior and "creativity." A fixed and universal curriculum will free educators to devote their ingenuity to matching the hordes of children with classrooms, educational hardware, and teaching functionaries.

The ultimate end of every expanding overpopulated, monolithic political and cultural entity has been some kind of totalitarianism. While the system and the numbers have varied depending on the geographical, ecological, and political circumstances, in all cases the aim of totalitarianism was to bring order out of disorder. It has always derived from society's inability to accommodate independence and variation in a context of egalitarianism and justice. The people of Rome were hardly aware that the character of their society was changing as the Republic grew larger and more powerful, expansive, and inchoate. As an imperial nation, Rome had a military and bureaucratic organization that continued as effectively as ever. But to support the vast apparatus, to control and renew its vast territories and populations drained the system of its last bit of initiative. Exploitation and authoritarianism grew as the inner fabric rotted. In the end the inner contradictions of this system caused its collapse.

In efficiency Rome's achievement was as miraculous as that of the pyramid builders of Egypt or the civil service of Confucian China. But in creativity, in vitality, in humanity, it could not touch ancient Athens or Alexandria, Gothic Paris, or Renaissance Florence and London, all relatively small urban environments. It might be helpful to judge these cities from the standpoint of their educational achievement. In each there was a balance between material satisfactions and a style of life which enhanced the personal, esthetic, and creative qualities of its citizens. In Rome the weight of numbers and the superimposition of hierarchical organizations to manage the whole militated irresistibly against the free-wheeling initiative that has characterized the most exciting eras in history.

There is a lesson here from evolution that might be worth extrapolating for our own use. Those species which have adapted or survived through quantity are endowed with the least individuality and the most specific instinctual assignments. Evolution, however, has provided room for other behavioral alternatives. The unique branch of life represented by the anthropoids is characterized by selection through individuation. A few individuals of high quality in each generation, carefully nurtured, led ultimately to the creation and the dominance of *Homo sapiens*. We are not Infusoria, ants, or lemmings.

Our concern for population structure therefore does not derive alone from considerations of economic and material deprivation. Humans need life space. The need is, of course, relative. The frontier farmer felt he was being crowded if he could see the smoke from a neighbor's fire or hear the barking of his dog across the hills. The medieval town was huddled house upon house. It was a symbolic refuge from the open lands—the manorial fields and wood lots—which lay outside the gates.

In our suburbs there are few open spaces, the houses are placed row on row, checkerboards of green symmetrically insulated and isolated. The spreading megalopolis of the East sprawling from Norfolk, Virginia to Portland, Maine and its concrete correlates in the mid- and far-West are a growing phenomenon. With each passing year the filth, noise, and congestion of the cities spread over their municipal boundaries. Violence and hysteria, stimulated by the mass media that envelop the people, that incite them to chain-reaction panics, ought to put us on guard.

The issue of the relationship between sheer weight of numbers and the various psychological and physiological breakdowns suffered by individuals is one that still has not been fully examined. However, there is an accumulation of evidence that would indicate that in the area of physical health alone, many of our new diseases, those which have not been as common in the past, may in some manner be related to the social conditions under which we live. Edward Deevey has described recent evidence that supports this hypothesis, using as examples mammals such as the rabbit, rat, and lemming.[2] Population of these animals has been known to increase for several years in a sharp incline, then suddenly, for no apparent ecological or competitive reason, they die off precipitously. These fluctuations have been noted to be a periodical phenomenon with a predictable rhythm of increase and then sudden decrease.

The analysis of rabbits and rats has been restricted to situations in which the animals had no egress, on islands. The lemmings' demographic gyrations are characterized every few years in their massive, suicidal march to the sea. An internal examination of these dead animals (rabbits and lemmings) showed widespread evidence of cirrhosis of the liver and hypertension, ailments that are not unknown to modern man. Deevey's conclusion, which echoes the general consensus, is that the animals died as a result of stress disease. The sensory excitement and overstimulation of being in close confinement with others

[2] Edward Deevey, "The Hare and the Haruspex," in Eric and Mary Josephson (eds.), *Man Alone* (New York: Dell Publishing Co., Inc., 1962).

of the same species, whether in the underground compartments of the lemmings or in the islands of the rabbits and rats, resulted in the internal breakdown of bodily functions on a vast scale.

We cannot go on populating the world at a rate determined only by the gross limits set by want and starvation. Not only does man need to live amidst an abundance of material and cultural artifacts to be able to freely exercise the possibility of choice, but he must have the physical room to breathe psychologically. The freedom to move about, change habitat, travel to refresh one's perception, to see and experience new things are uncomplicated but basic necessities. In an expanding and uniform megalopolis they become impossible. The highways, and even more so the "flyways," make travel and movement not only a terrifying experience, but when one arrives at a destination, is there anything new worth viewing?

Whether or not the sociologist Robert Dahl is correct that the maximum size of any community ought to be at most 200,000 people, it must be true that the urban conglomerates are becoming impossible to govern, clean, and police without the imposition of the severest of personal restrictions. Yet is it so inconceivable to hypothesize that in our technologically ingenious world the material satisfactions of our population, the retention of our standard of living, and the preservation of our democratic forms and values can be maintained without the massive production and consumption mythology to which we have committed ourselves?

The world population may be seven billion by the year 2000, roughly double its present total. There are some who, on the basis of this specter, would argue the impossibility of any but the most ameliorative policies for both the United States and the world in general. Thus, rather than pattern ourselves for a more complete democratic social life, we might better arm economically to save ourselves. Yet there has to be a pattern for the world to follow. And if we are the most advanced state, this is our opportunity to become a showcase of human possibilities for the benefit of mankind. There is thus a measure of justification for national autonomies. Neither for historic or judicial reasons is there any need for one nation to suffer for the endemic deficiencies or social errors of others.

If, let us say, a nation like Denmark can achieve a rational balance between natural resources and population, it ought not suffer for the myopia of any neighboring society. It and we, within our capacities, should aid all nations of the world to bring reason to the problems of demography, ecology, and technology—issues crucial to social planning in the context of a peaceful world order.

As it is, the United States is still an interdependent and federated structure. Thus Vermont must suffer for the excesses of New Jersey and New York, and vice versa. As long as we still have time for trial-and-error patterns of reform, it is doubtful that we will hear the rumblings of secession. But if urbanization continues apace, we should not be surprised to hear some very cogent arguments about rationality, world opinion, and distributive justice geared to this plea.

The heart of our argument revolves around the fact that medical technology has now made possible voluntary controls over family size. The problem of human increase is now subject to rational public intervention without war, pestilence, or famine. True, we speak in terms of societies that are acknowledgedly advanced. Yet it is not beyond possibility that advances in the next few years will allow radically underdeveloped nations to efficiently control population growth.

The problem of human rights and freedoms enters precisely at this point. What we tentatively suggest is a twofold approach to this issue of family planning. It would be a preliminary means of retarding or stopping the increase in our population so that we might gain a measure of control over our social and educational destinies. If government can economically favor those having many children, then it can favor those having few or none. The tax laws are a clear way of benefiting those who wish to have no children or have at most one or two children.

For those parents who choose to submit themselves to the obligations and satisfactions of raising a larger family, the state has no economic responsibility. On the contrary, society has a right to assure itself of the well-being of every child. The position is not as hard or inhuman as it sounds. In the first place, we have enough awareness of child development, at least in the context of the modern Western family, to assert certain prerequisites for the rearing of socially useful citizens. The day of the extended or tribal family is gone. In the past, hordes of children were cared for by various grandparents, aunts, cousins, and older brothers and sisters, as well as by parents. This situation is likewise past. The responsibilities inherent in the nuclear family are crucial. It is doubtful that any but the super-rich can pay for the child care that half a dozen children necessitate. We cannot afford the casual child-rearing patterns of the indifferent or the poverty stricken. And it is doubtful that child-care centers or nurseries are the answer.

However, if we do not decide to benefit financially those who wish to raise large families, we ought not penalize the child. There is no reason why a substantial set of credits could not be provided for the child in the form of complete medical and social services, clothing, furniture, and school equipment. The school itself, private or public, could become an institution through which a variety of necessities could be provided—hot meals, medical and social care, books and equipment. If we instituted such a plan, the option of child rearing would possibly be chosen by a smaller proportion of the population. We might even be able to achieve a better percentage of responsible parents and necessarily healthier and contributing young citizens.

Could we not live just as well, just as safely and luxuriously in a society of 75 to 100 million people as in a nation of 300 million? And would not the United States be a more interesting and educationally suitable environment if we would focus on people as persons rather than statistics and numbers? Could we not renew our communities periodically, control our wastes, develop truly open spaces between our cities, cities which would have opportunities to create the character and uniqueness that we prize and talk so much about in our literature about old New Orleans, San Francisco, and Boston?

Self-management—the participatory democracy envisioned in the Port Huron Statement of the Students for a Democratic Society—seems to be a legitimate enunciation of a fundamental social need for man. But in addition to entertaining such wonderful aspirations, we must prepare the structural groundwork for such an ideal. If we have indeed retreated from the legendary democratic forms of the early-nineteenth-century small town, it is because of the social changes which have occurred.

To cry for participatory democracy, for decentralization, even for pluralism, in a society of 200 to 300 million people or more is to delude oneself. These ends cannot be achieved. The organizational requirements to provide us with the basic necessities preclude much individual initiative outside the existing corporate hierarchies.

THE EDUCATIONAL ISSUE

The issue of overpopulation is basic. The hope for a humane democratic pluralism is an illusion if this trend is not halted and indeed rolled back. This is not a job of a score of years. It is a process which, even if pressed by far more people than now, will take a century or more. But if accomplished on a world-wide basis, a necessary but hardly imminent prospect, it would do more to insure peace among men than a dozen United Nations.

A host of social actions needs to be taken in the direction of presenting living alternatives to the megalopolis. Communities as Reston, Virginia and Columbia, Maryland are important in that they represent such living alternatives. They reflect a conscious attempt to use reason in building into a structure of community life the opportunities needed by people to create a controllable social environment.

But our major concern is the educational context. For here is demonstrated the most recent and articulated unease with the state of things. Perhaps it is a pious hope for the educationist to believe that there is here more possibility for effecting change than in the business, labor, or governmental areas. But we only need first steps if our assumption about the trend towards decentralization is correct. And since education is concerned primarily with the young, and since it is a virtue of the young that they are as yet uncommitted and unsatiated, then it is logical that we begin with them.

Rights of Students

The wave of student revolts which started in colleges such as the University of California in the mid-1960's and spread to numerous other large institutions, both domestic and foreign, reflects a new era, an era of awareness by the college student of the sociological fact of his existence as an important group or class in our society. For the most part, students have had little command over the conditions under which they must function. Only recently have they become aware of the manner in which they are being exploited by institutions whose concern increasingly lies elsewhere. The educational institutions have been the target in a general seduction, along with business, labor, philanthropy, art, by the governmental hegemony. Education is no different in the ascendancy of the system builders—those administrators who gravitate toward the centers of power, the research liaison with defense, the catering to business for corporate support, and the competition for size, wealth, and prestige, which have turned many universities into gigantic corporate enterprises or states within a state.

Under such conditions, the student comes as something of an afterthought. One cannot point with pride to an educated, humanized individual as easily and unequivocally as one can to a new building or to the gross size of the overall enterprise. A ledger of student learning does not read as well as a ledger showing endowment growth or research grants. Paul Goodman has rightly characterized the entire endeavor as one that processes students rather than educates them.

The strikes, the invasion of administrative offices, the general agitation are a product of a malaise, a disenchantment with the overall course of national concerns, whether in foreign adventures or in warped domestic priorities. They have initiated a time of turmoil. But the fact that there exists a committed and aware minority of students that knows it is being cheated of an important set of educational values is ground for hope that the system can be moved.

These students feel the need to participate in the decisions that must affect them. They demand only that the university fly its colors clearly. They want to know: to what is the university committed, to what kind of research; where are the professors whose names in the catalogues brought students to the institution in the first place; how can an education of involvement, personal recognition and responsibility be obtained in institutions of fifteen, twenty, or thirty thousand students? Issues such as the responsibility of a Columbia or Chicago to the surrounding community are crucial to the status of the university as a humanizing and educational institution. So, too, are such short-run reforms as faculty senates and elimination of compromising military research assignments.

But perhaps even more important is the right of students to attend institutions, if for example they so wish, with a maximum size of 5,000, a maximum ratio of teaching faculty to students of, say, one to ten. It is a legitimate right. The American Federation of Teachers has been negotiating contracts that include average class sizes in order to inhibit penurious school boards and manipulating administrations from foisting on helpless teachers far more students than they can handle. Here the teachers have taken the initiative.

In the case of the college, the professor is usually willing to relent on this point; he will tolerate large numbers of students to get some time off to do research, which means much more to his career than teaching. It is the student here who must stand firm for his educational rights. Not only general ratios of teaching faculty to students, but also class size and student-faculty contact opportunities ought to be negotiable.

It is natural, using cost-efficiency charts derived from the manufacture of canned soups or automobiles, to think of institutional planning in terms of universities of twenty to thirty thousand students or more. State legislatures, likewise cost conscious, tend to support this kind of thinking. Fortunately those students and teachers who now judge the relative efficiency of the large institutions are animate, independent human beings, with no vested interest in the particular structure of their institutions.

It is difficult to believe that this generation of students, or those of the future, will support the supposed economic efficiency of a Berkeley or Ohio State. It is not Utopian to suggest that a student have the right in every state to choose institutions of various demographic characteristics, from 3,000 down to 750 students. No parent of an elementary school child would tolerate his child attending an institution of 2,000 pupils. Sound educational reasoning would likewise place limits on the size of institutions of higher learning.

Local Control

For generations Americans have been committed to a belief that local control over the schools represents an important bastion of democracy. This belief has been accepted at a time when local control has been increasingly divested of its once vaunted autonomy. As Kimball and McClellan have put it,

> Even the belief that education remains a local function proves on careful inspection to be merely a comforting illusion. State legislators have long since placed educational control in state boards and departments of education, the teaching profession establishes the ethics governing activities within the classroom, and textbook publishers (in conjunction with makers of standardized tests) determine the content of instruction. The interrelation of many different kinds of corporate organizations—public, private (profit and non-profit), and voluntary professions—are seen clearly in their impact on the community's education. This is typical of community life in general.[3]

The general trend away from local control has taken place in the belief that small communities would refuse to appropriate requisite funds for the support of education, would require indifferent standards of achievement and might engage in subprofessional practices with regard to both students and teachers. During the eras of our shift from rural to industrial patterns the inequalities in education perhaps needed controlling. But today surely the interrelatedness of things, the efficiency of communications and transportation have brought all parts of our country closer together and evened out many differences. The question of local autonomy now revolves around new sets of priorities and needs. Control has fallen increasingly into state and professional hands, and citizens are becoming more aware than ever of the usurpation of rights that ought to be reserved to parents.

The arguments of the state in its appropriation of controls have varied from era to era. In the recent past the rationalization has been the need to centralize for the sake of developing more modern (defense) curricula and school facilities. Today the state argues it needs control to restructure districts that were gerrymandered in attempts to resegregate black children, or it needs control to dissolve neighborhood schools in favor of a racially heterogeneous student distribution. As the state acts to regulate and as teachers become increasingly militant and independent, the specter of ultimate federal intrusion comes closer.

[3] *Education and the New America* (New York: Random House, Inc., 1962), p. 205.

Our concern is not merely to bring about local control for its own sake. The state and federal authorities ought not be interpreted solely as usurpers. What we are concerned with is that under the aegis of very respectable egalitarian and scientific principles in education practical issues will be resolved, but in the process sets of rigid regulations will have been created that will now be imposed and maintained for their own sake.

By rationalizing, by explicitly setting forth the rights of the larger society and balancing them against the legitimate retention of independent action in the community, we might achieve legal adjudication of the universal and plural interests of all involved. Basically no child ought to suffer educational deprivation wherever he is educated, whether in Mississippi or Massachusetts. Thus there should be no occasion for local penury to necessitate outside intervention. The nation owes every child an equal opportunity. Likewise it would seem correct that the kind of rational intelligence we deem necessary for participation in a world society and exemplified in certain scientific and social areas of the curriculum could likewise be mandated and supervised universally, at the same time, flexibly.

As we have pointed out with regard to our minorities and in reference to the nondiscursive elements of the curriculum, there are plural rights, in this case, the freedom of diverse groups to represent their culture within the curriculum. This kind of freedom ought to be specifically delegated to the local, decentralized school district. In cases where minorities are found, even within fairly small districts, some sort of pragmatic solution could be worked out. Such a case should pose no insoluble problems when men are aware of the democratic grounds upon which the discussion is taking place. Too often the state has resolved such issues with coercion, the community expressing its weakness in limp assent.

By centering our concern for the rights of minorities on their community status and on the issue of local control and decentralization, new opportunities could be opened up. Legitimately we ought not favor white over black, Mexican over Indian. Nondiscrimination of individual by individual works both ways. Racial quotas of any kind are anathema. On the other hand we have long respected the principle that some communities need more help than others. We have assigned defense contracts, built atomic installations, post offices, military bases,

TVA's, all in the name of giving a helping hand to the more unfortunate. Were educational assistance rendered to needy *communities*, the ethnic or racial homogeneity of the communities would be an incidental feature of the aid. And of course this is what is being done in the various federal programs.

Some might argue that with our population already over 200 million and likely to go higher, inviting local communities to develop their own curricular and structural approaches would be courting educational anarchy. However, to agree to centralization on this argument would be like subjecting mentally healthy nurses and doctors to the rules of an institution for the mentally ill.

The rights of local communities must take priority over the supposed and ineluctable practical needs for regulating numbers, especially when, as is now the case, the numbers can be decreased. We would, in addition, suggest that members of any region or locality have the right to split into an independent school district if the school population exceeds a given size. Whether the size is conceived in terms of several moderate-size elementary schools, a junior and senior high school, and even a shared community college, is an open question, subject to real practical exigency. But we do not envision a high school building housing four to six thousand students, a situation we occasionally see in our larger cities. If people so will it, they can join with other districts to develop special programs. The democratic principle here is that the state and federal governments exist to serve the needs of communities, needs which further the communities' own exercise of freedom.

We are protected today from the extreme idiosyncratic errors that could have developed years ago under local control. Society has many subtle social avenues available for the buffering of extreme difference. The mass media, modern transport, the opportunity for all men to scrutinize the choices each locale might make, all inhibit the development of radically antisocial trends. Even so, freedom needs for its exercise room to make mistakes, as long as they affect only their perpetrator.

Private Education

There are many precarious shoals that must be avoided before local control and autonomy can be expanded. One of these, the role of the federal government in education, looms large in any picture of tomorrow's education. The federal government has barely touched the lower schools with its beneficence. Often support for these programs has tended to go directly to the local community, bypassing, to their chagrin, the state and city governments. But one important qualification remains. The Department of Health, Education and Welfare is unlikely to give monies carte blanche without making specific substantive requirements for their use. And given the random, sometimes capricious manner of granting federal largess, it is not likely that the monies will be given on the basis of the right of the local community, but rather as a specific philanthropic dispensation by those who hold the ultimate power. The historic polarization of power between the state and the individual will, to that extent, be exacerbated.

In New York City a decentralization plan ratified by the State (mid 1969) marked the conclusion of several years of strife between extremely polarized segments of the community. The tragic irrationality engendered, the racial hate, violence, and raw power plays have done much to shake the foundation of the school system. That a decentralization plan to divide the City into thirty or forty districts could yet be promulgated indicates the depth of the support for local participation and control. Yet, can it be denied that these modest structural alignments will not go far in producing diversity? The shadow of city, state, and federal power should darken the hopes of even the most ardent and optimistic espousers of qualitative differentiation within public education.

The grasping of independence in developing a modicum of educational initiative may take place so slowly in our local communities and with such protracted efforts that it might be strategic to shift some of our effort to support of the private school. Our concern is with progress in developing more meaningful educational programs. As in all things the enemy of progress is vested interests. The private schools may be a source of innovation and competition, enough so to stimulate some changes in the larger public domain.

We have advanced far beyond the misguided attempts to destroy private education and force everyone into the public school. The watershed Oregon decision of 1925 guaranteed the

the production of a mechanistic, meritocratic mentality. It has resulted in the Educational Testing Service of Princeton, New Jersey, becoming the arbiter of what constitutes the conventional knowledge of our nation.[6]

CONCLUSION

We have here presented an argument for cultural pluralism in an educational context wherein pluralism would be nurtured rather than extinguished, as it was in a former period. We have emphasized the fact that there is an inherently pluralistic thrust in knowledge and culture which must have its social envisionment. The futility of modern American education in the context of a vast bureaucratized and centralized corporate system to a great degree reflects the unnatural desiccation of those basic and intrinsic pluralistic and nondiscursive communitarian rights of man.

Ultimately man will have to face intellectually the issues of equality, universality, and plurality. They are not easy or simple educational issues. Complicating any hope for a pat equation between these dynamic and seemingly antithetical elements in human thought are the ever-present issues of scarcity and distribution in all segments of a world society, the need to fulfill innovative cultures without denigrating more placid and static societies, and the need to keep options open for various rates of advance, possibly even to slow down rapidly differentiating and disintegrating societies. Many problems lie ahead, even with the not too eager acceptance by the world community of a principle of universal equality in difference.

One thing is sure: the world will not see the vast differences in cultural patterns that it once did and that so bedeviled traditional American educators. The day of total cultural incommensurability and untranslatability is over. In that sense it is a world society our grandchildren are destined to inhabit. Margaret Mead has beautifully described an example of the world of the past which will have disappeared in a few generations.[7]

[6] See Charles Benson, *The Cheerful Prospect* (Boston: Houghton Mifflin Company, 1965), p. 114, where Benson as a means for bringing about equality in education suggests that all reading teachers be qualified through ETS examination. This "cheerful prospect" is pursued diligently throughout the book.

[7] Margaret Mead, *Sex and Temperament in Three Primitive Societies* (New York: William Morrow & Co., Inc., 1963).

In New Guinea lived three tribes, the Arapesh, the Mundugumor, and the Tchambuli. They were only a few minutes apart by airplane, but in the impenetrable jungles, these tribes were eons apart in their cultures, traditions, and slant on life. The Arapesh—peaceful, almost feminine in their attitudes toward what they considered a continuously receptive world; the Mundugumor—fierce headhunters, viciously competetive to the point of making women into "men" and perverting the traditional parent-child relationships; the Tchambuli—artistic, almost schizophrenic, touched by white civilization and thereby saved from extinction, intrinsically different from the other two. These peoples were all of the same basic Melanesian stock, yet they might as well have been Eskimoes, Arabs, and Hindi to each other.

These kinds of differences we will have lost. We might compare the pluralism of tomorrow to an undulating wave. In traditional terms, differences and historical changes in culture could be visualized through the slow frequency of undulations, the great amplitude of the swells pulsating languidly on either side of the axis. The future will show a far more rapid frequency of cultural change in our world, but the amplitude will be drastically reduced. The changes, rapid but small in dimension, will also have one other altered quality. Whereas in primitive or traditional societies, the materials of cultural change were few—cultures being so impoverished in the variety of symbols, artifacts, and institutions—the future will bring before man a vast repertoire of materials, institutional patterns of life, technology, art, even personality configuration. All of these will present choice of a variety never before thought possible.

The palette of cultural change will be limited in extent and variety only by man's imagination and will. Here lies the essential mystery of the educational process. It will not matter in what direction civilizational advance will have led us earlier. The fanning out of ever new diversities will be a product of the conscious choices made by each generation. Freedom will then demand that the old generation keep the options open for the choices of the new. Education will necessitate that the young be taught to choose their deviations wisely. What system of education will be courageous enough to accept such a mission?

Index